Origami

PELHAM CRAFT SERIES

Origami

GEORGIE DAVIDSON

PELHAM BOOKS

First published in Great Britain by
PELHAM BOOKS LTD
52 Bedford Square
London W.C.1
1975

ISBN 0 7207 0758 7

Filmset in 10/12pt Univers Medium and printed by
BAS Printers Limited, Wallop, Hampshire
and bound by Dorstel Press, Harlow.

Contents

Illustrations

Symbols

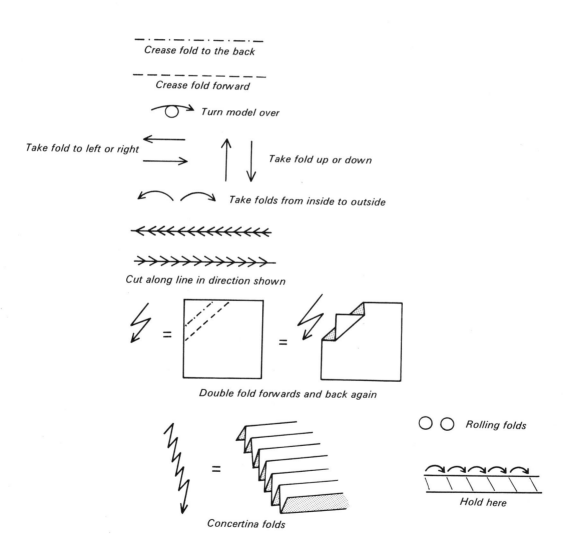

———·——·——·——·——·——·——
Crease fold to the back

——————————
Crease fold forward

Turn model over

Take fold to left or right

Take fold up or down

Take folds from inside to outside

Cut along line in direction shown

Double fold forwards and back again

Concertina folds

Rolling folds

Hold here

CHAPTER 1

The Craft – and the Paper Shapes

The word 'Origami' is a Japanese one and most of the development in the art of paper folding is accredited to Japanese people. Although in other countries paper folding has been done since the advent of paper, the universally accepted word for this type of work remains the Japanese one, and the majority of Masters and leading folders are Japanese. Models are attributed to the Masters who invented them and every enthusiast seeks to go down to posterity with a fantastic discovery to his credit. Alas all too often the supposed new discovery turns out to have been made before. The most one can perhaps expect to achieve, in this age when paper is so plentiful and people of all ages are experimenting with it, is a new use of established folds. When paper was a luxury it was used in Japan only on ceremonial occasions, and it is not until the twelfth century that records show models of animals. One of the oldest of the ceremonially used folds still existing and in use today is the 'noshi'. This is a small ornament of folded paper which shops in Japan still attach to a purchase when they know it is for a gift. Its use expresses the hope that the recipient will enjoy good fortune. The actual noshi is a long stem of abalone which is placed inside the folded paper, the whole being fastened together by a narrow band or cord.

The oldest and most complicated model seems to be the Crab – it can be traced back to a Master in the twelfth century. The model is made from a triangle of paper – most probably because this was the most economical shape at that time when paper was made from straw and very rare. The straw paper was also very strong and could, therefore, support the very involved folds used.

In this book I have tried to place the models in groups for possible use. This does not mean, however, that one should only make Origami when one has a practical use for it – far from it. Its greatest quality lies in its therapeutic benefits for, while making models, one can, as with many of the other creative media, concentrate and relax, and in this way reach tranquillity.

Partly because I watched a small child discard its more sophisticated toys and become absorbed in playing with a paper plane, and partly because I know their value as exercises in folding, I have included a few of the childhood favourites. Also in the back of my mind was the memory of an article, read in an airline magazine on a flight to somewhere or other, that told the story of the development of a new style of aircraft from ideas gathered by a father when watching his son play with folded paper planes. This brings us to another of the good points of Origami – its use as a creative medium. The Masters of hundreds of years ago experimented and devised a number of basic folds; from these folds all models derive, albeit by different routes. The good folder will want to practise and become very

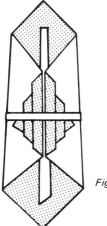

Figure 1. Noshi

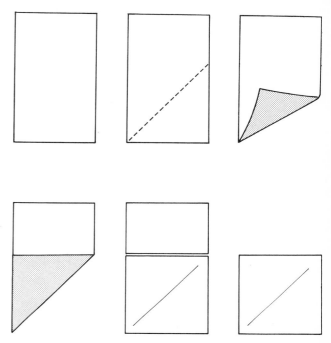

Figure 2. Making a square from a rectangle

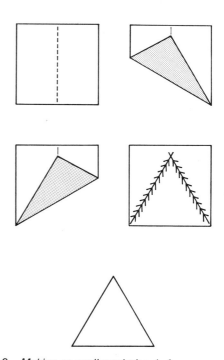

Figure 3. Making an equilateral triangle from a square

efficient in folding them, for he will realise that in these lies the key to the whole art.

Origami paper is paper which has one side brightly coloured and the other white. Regrettably it is neither cheap nor easy to obtain. Sealed packets, moreover, often contain paper of very inferior quality — so care should be taken. Because of these problems I have experimented with other papers, and have found that in an average household a very good selection of suitable paper can be found. You should, however, avoid paper with cracks and, especially if working with children, that which has fine but sharp edges. I have found that tissue paper — this is obtainable in many colours — is excellent for small and blow-up models. Packing paper in brown, dark green and blue is strong and excellent for compound models such as the camel and the reindeer — it stands very well. Foil-covered paper of a heavy quality was used for the dragon and for the reindeer in the Christmas table set. Newspaper, shelf paper and carbon copy paper were invaluable. The crêpe papers and embossed papers were acceptable for masks, but the models look a little clumsy. The poorer quality paper napkin can be used, but not for meticulous folding.

As mentioned earlier, the first paper shape used was the triangle; the famous crab is folded from this. It was followed by the square which allowed greater scope for geometrical

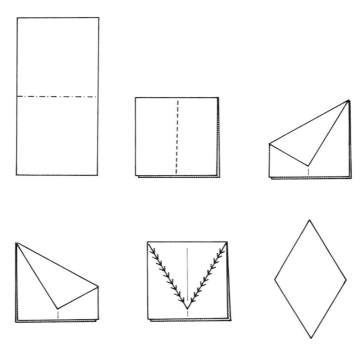

Figure 4. Making a rhombus

shapes. Other world-famous figures include the bat with outstretched wings, folded from rhombic shaped paper, and the turtle from hexagonal. Pentagonal and octagonal shapes were used mostly for flowers and ornaments. It is interesting to note that the only shape included in a normal packet of origami paper today is the square. You must make the other shapes from that. It might seem pedantic to say that a square must have perfect corners, but you will find yourself at such a great disadvantage if you start off with a bad one. Diagram 2 shows how to reach a square from a rectangle ; diagrams 3 and 4 show how to make an equilateral triangle from a square, and how to make a rhombus from a rectangle made from a double square.

Having made your paper into an acceptable shape, now follow the exercises in creasing by making these seemingly simple models. The finished shapes may amuse the young, but their principal use is to make you an accurate folder able to control your paper. If possible use a flat surface to fold on — match up the points carefully and make the folds by creasing from the middle out to the left/right returning to the middle and then out to the right/left.

CHAPTER 2

First Exercises

Crease folding is of the utmost importance for well finished models. Although the models or shapes, as perhaps they should be called, may amuse small children or be suitable for collages, that is not the reason behind their inclusion. Their great use is in showing you the great value of crease folds, the great potential and strength of paper, to train you to fold carefully and precisely, and to awaken you to the creative possibilities of a square of paper. The first exercises are based on straight folds and the second group on diagonal.

 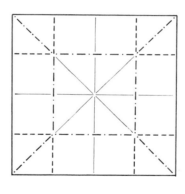 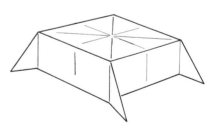

Figure 5. Table cloth with mitred corners

Table Cloth with Mitred Corners
This cloth with set corners will help you achieve accuracy in your folding and emphasises the value of forward and backward crease folds. With the face of the paper towards you make horizontal, vertical and diagonal creases. The diagonal creases will quarter the paper into triangles and the vertical and horizontal creases will divide it into sixteen equal squares.
1. Plain square.
2. Crease folds have been made.
3. Use the four centre squares as a table top and fold the corners using the diagonal folds.

13

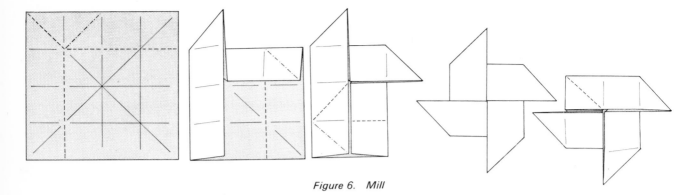

Figure 6. Mill

Mill

Open out table cloth or crease another square in similar fashion.

1. Opened-out paper — wrong side towards you.
2. Fold in, on crease lines, the left-hand and top edges, leaving the original top left corner extended.
3. Fold in right-hand side — top right corner will be extended.
4. Fold up lower edge — the lower right- and left-hand corners will now be left extended and the mill will be completed.

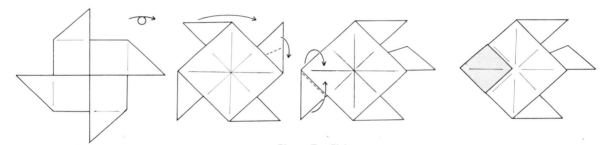

Figure 7. Fish

Fish

1. Commence with Mill model.
2. Turn model over and to position shown. Reverse the direction of the top flap to make a fin. Crease fold flap on the right to form a tail.
3. Fold in tail section on crease fold made.

Crease fold the flap on the left to both right and left sides to facilitate folding it back to form a contrastingly coloured head. (See diagram 32)
4. Fold the head section over the body — this sort of outside fold is known as a hood fold — and you have a fish.

Vase

1. Commence with the Mill shape.
2. Crease fold model in half along line indicated, making the fold to the back.
3. Lift right and left side flaps up.
4. A vase for collage work.

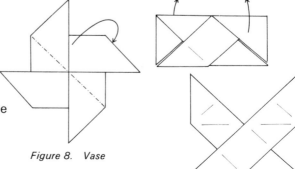

Figure 8. Vase

Double Boat

1. Commence with Vase shape.
2. Half turn the model and crease and fold what has become the flap at the top forward and down on the line shown.
3. Take the right-hand flap behind and across to that on the left-hand side. This will bring up the lower flaps. Pull them out to the right and a double boat has been formed.
4. Finished boat.

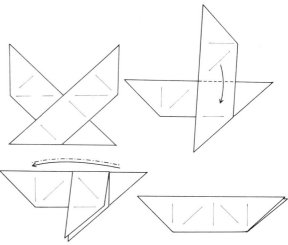

Figure 9.   Double boat

Boat with Sail

1. Commence with Vase shape turned to the left. Crease fold on line shown.
2. Bring lower flap up and to the right to form a boat with a sail.

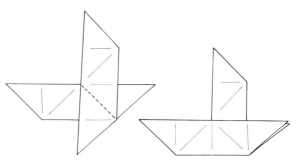

Figure 10.   Boat with sail

Bird

1. Commence with Boat with Sail. Crease fold flaps on the right-hand side on line indicated — one to the back and one to the front.
2. Fold down flaps on crease lines made. Crease fold the top point on the line shown, taking the point both to the back and to the front to facilitate the folding of the head.
3. Fold the top point down and over to form a head (a hood fold). Crease fold a small section to form a tail — on the line indicated.
4. Fold in the tail section on crease made — this inner type of fold is known as a pocket fold (see Diagram 31). Add spot for eye.

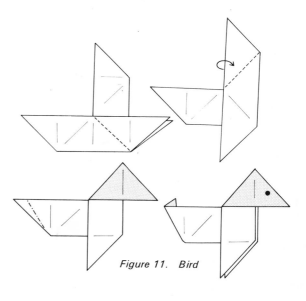

Figure 11.   Bird

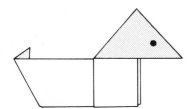

Figure 12.   Duck

Duck

Commence with Bird. Crease and fold the wings to the inside.

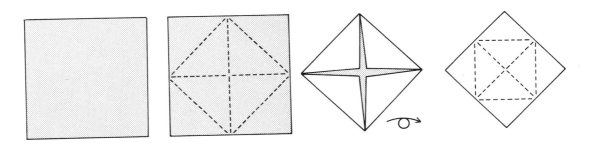

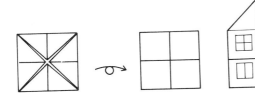

Figure 13. House

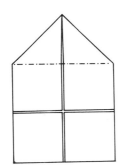 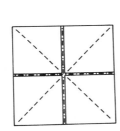 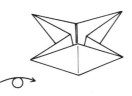

House
1. Take a plain square of paper.
2. Crease fold as indicated.
3. Fold corners into the centre.
4. Turn model over, crease on lines shown.
5. Fold corners in to the centre.
6. Turn model over.
7. Lift top flap and decorate house.

Figure 14. Small container or guessing toy

Small Container or Guessing Toy
1. Commence with House (undecorated). Fold down roof section.
2. Crease fold as indicated and turn over. Then insert a finger under each of the four central points and press model into shape as 3.
4. Model standing as a small container. Decorate or number the inner sections of the lower points if you wish to use it as a guessing game.

Thread Holder
1. Commence with a plain square. Find centre by folding paper into quarters.
2. Fold corners to centre.
3. Turn model over and again fold corners to centre.
4. Turn model over and again fold corners to centre.
5. Turn model over and lift centre points up and out to their respective corners opening and flattening them by applying light pressure.
6. Finished thread holder.

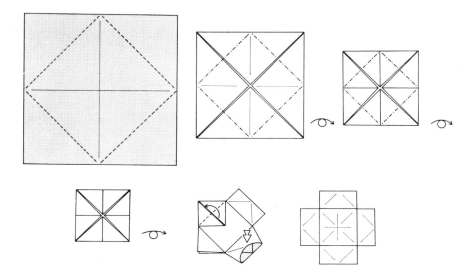

Figure 15. Thread holder

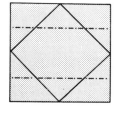

Figure 16. Chair and table

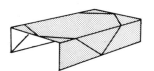

Chair and Table
1. Commence with Thread Holder, and fold three sides down and one side up to form a chair.
2. Fold four sides down to form a table.

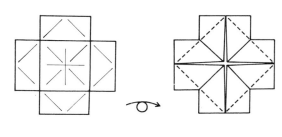

Figure 17. Long table

Long Table
1. Commence with Thread Holder.
2. Turn model over and take centre points out to their respective sides.
3. Crease fold on lines shown.
4. Fold upper and lower edges down to form a long table.

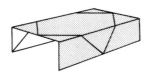 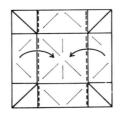  

Figure 18. Double boat

Double Boat
1. Commence with Long Table.
2. Turn model over and flatten. Bring the two sides to meet in the centre using the creases already made.

3. When this is accomplished apply gentle pressure and bring the two edges to meet and fold in lower point to form keel.
4. A double boat will have been formed.

Double Boat with Sail
1. Commence with Double Boat.
2. Pull the flaps tucked inside, on long sides of boat, up and out to form sails.

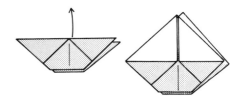

Figure 19. Double boat with sail

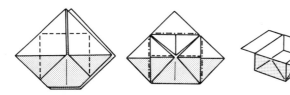

Figure 20. Box

Box
1. Commence with Double Boat with Sails. Fold sides and top forward to meet in centre.
2. Fold down on line shown. Turn model over and repeat folds on other side.
3. Open model out by gently pulling double ends apart. A small container or box has now emerged.

By now you should be conversant with the folds and have confidence in your folding. Continue with these basic forms creating simple models by yourself. Picture frames, gondolas and other boxes will come very easily.

18

CHAPTER 3

Basic Folds

In doing the exercises in the previous chapters, you have learnt to appreciate the possibilities and potential of a square of paper, the importance of precise folding, and have doubtless been amazed at the strength and durability of it as a material. We now proceed to the Basic Folds. These have been used over the ages as foundations for the more classical models.

Fold the more complicated ones until you can make them perfectly. There are a number of different routes that can be followed to the same end — left-handed persons, people with fingers less agile than thumbs, all can adapt to their own requirements providing the correct basic shape emerges at the end. One of my ideas of luxury is to pick up my Origami folder and find it well stocked with basic folds, for when you feel in an experimental mood it is far better to take a separate basic fold for each step than to go from first to last with one piece of paper — it is almost impossible to retrace your steps quickly and accurately and who knows — a new model may have been lost to posterity.

All of the basic folds are started with the wrong side of the paper towards you. When the exception to this rule occurs the notes for the particular model will make it clear.

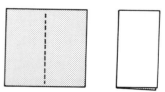

Figure 21. Basic Fold One

BASIC FOLD ONE — the Rectangle Book Fold
1. Place wrong side of paper towards you.
2. Fold paper in half carefully, aligning sides and matching the corners.
3. Crease first in the middle of the folded edge taking the fold up, returning to the centre and then down.

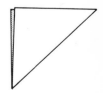

Figure 22. Basic Fold Two

BASIC FOLD TWO — the Triangle
1. Place wrong side of paper towards you.
2. Take the lower right point up to meet the top left one.
3. Align edges carefully and crease along the folded edge being careful to make the creases from the centre to the sides.

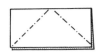

Figure 23.   Basic Fold Three

BASIC FOLD THREE — a Double Triangle

1. With the wrong side of the paper towards you, crease fold the diagonal lines shown on the diagram forwards — this is indicated by the simple broken line — the horizontal line should be folded to the back — indicated by a broken line interspersed with dots.

2. In spite of the backward crease, fold the paper in half by bringing the top section forward and down, keeping the right side of the paper on the outside.

3. Using light pressure direct the top left- and right-hand corners down between the front and back layers. This inside fold is, incidentally, called a pocket fold when used on a model. A double triangle will have been formed, opening at the bottom. This is a popular basic fold for simple models of birds in flight as it gives both a wing span and the possibility of forming a body.

Figure 24.   Basic Fold Four

BASIC FOLD FOUR — often called a Fish Base

Popular for birds such as swans, ducks, etc. depicted as being on water and modern style 'block' animals such as the hen, chick, dog, elephant. This base allows no possibilities for legs.

1. Place the wrong side of the paper towards you.

2. To establish a centre line, crease fold the lower right-hand corner up to meet that at the top left. Open out and fold lower and left edges forward to meet this centre line.

3. Finished basic fold.

Figure 25.   Basic Fold Five

BASIC FOLD FIVE

Used for table napkins, some boxes, baskets, flowers, etc.

1. Place the wrong side of the paper towards you.

2. Crease fold into quarters as shown — this will find the true centre for you.

3. Crease fold corners in to meet the centre crease.

4. Fold the corners in to meet in the centre.

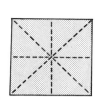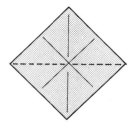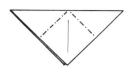

Figure 26. Basic Fold Six

BASIC FOLD SIX — a Double Square

This fold is the halfway stage to the more complicated forms which follow, the great difference being in whether the open or the closed edges are folded to the centre.

1. Place wrong side of paper towards you.
2. Crease fold paper into quarters by folding top half forward and down over the bottom half, opening it out folding the right side forward and over to the left and then by taking the lower right-hand corner forward and up to meet the top left and vice-versa.
3. Turn the paper to position shown.
4. Fold paper in half by bringing the top point forward and down to meet the point at the bottom. Crease fold left- and right-hand points to the back on lines shown.
5. Using slight pressure, push the right- and left-hand points down between the front and back sections — this is known as a pocket fold. You will now have two perfect squares joined by centre creases.

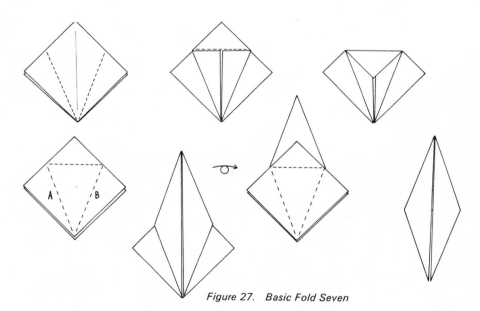

Figure 27. Basic Fold Seven

BASIC FOLD SEVEN

This is probably the most-used basic fold of all. Follow the instructions for Basic Fold Six through its five stages.

1. Keep the basic fold to the position shown, with open edges on the lower sides. Crease fold the lower right- and left-hand sides forward and across to meet in the centre.
2. Fold these edges in.
3. Fold down the top point as indicated.
4. Open model out again as shown.
5. Lift the top layer of the lower points forward and up, reversing crease folds A and B, until the paper falls into the shape shown.

6. Turn model over and crease fold forward on lines indicated.

7. Repeat the folding and lifting process using the top layer. You will now have two narrow points at the bottom and two wide points at the top.

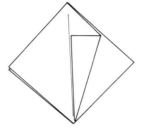

Figure 28. Basic Fold Eight

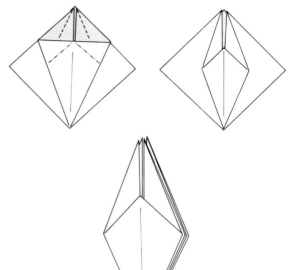

BASIC FOLD EIGHT

Follow the instructions for Basic Fold Six through its five stages and turn.

1. Crease fold the closed edges of the top layer of folds on the right-hand side of the model forward and in to the centre.

2. Lift the flap, made by the earlier crease, up and by applying light pressure flatten it so that it falls on either side as shown. Crease fold open ends of top layer of model forwards and down to meet in the centre. Release the creases and lift the straight edges of the earlier fold up so that they can fall into folds under it as indicated in the next diagram.

3. When the first flap has been refolded as shown, repeat the folds on the three other flaps.

4. When the folds are completed the finished Basic Fold Eight should have four points at the top and one at the bottom.

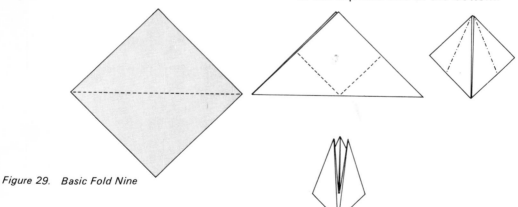

Figure 29. Basic Fold Nine

BASIC FOLD NINE

1. Place the wrong side of the paper towards you and crease fold forward on the line indicated.

2. Fold paper in half by taking the lower point up to meet the top. Crease fold the left- and right-hand points forward and up to meet the top point.

3. Fold the sides in on crease lines. Crease fold the open edges in again to meet in the centre. Open out the crease lines again.

4. Using slight pressure fold the left- and right-hand corners in so that a valley is formed between the front and back sections of the model.

From these basic folds you should be able to create compound or single models, quadrupeds or animals, decorations, masks — so many things — learn them thoroughly and from them create your own origami.

THE FOLDING FOR ARMS AND LEGS

Arms and legs are fashioned from hood and pocket folds. A pocket fold is a fold that goes to the inside of the model and a Hood fold is one that is folded over the outside of the model. Both of these folds are more easily accomplished if the paper is crease folded forwards and then backwards. To make yourself conversant with these folds practise the following exercises.

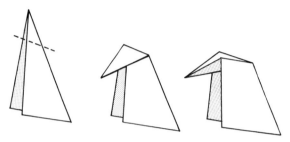
Figure 30. Bird's head — simple pocket fold

Bird's Head — Simple Pocket Fold

1. Crease fold both to the back and to the front on line indicated.
2. Fold as shown forward and down. Straighten model.
3. Hold the tip firmly and pull the section down and to the inside. This is a pocket fold.

Bird's Head — Simple Hood Fold

1. Crease fold on line indicated both to the back and to the front.
2. Fold as shown forward and down. Straighten model.
3. Hold the tip firmly and opening the fold slightly pull it down over the model. This is a hood fold.

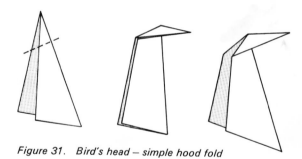
Figure 31. Bird's head — simple hood fold

Foot — Simple Hood Fold

1. Keep the folded edge of the leg on the side of the required foot. Crease fold on line indicated.
2. Fold as shown forward and across. Straighten out leg.
3. Holding the tip firmly pull the fold over.

Foot — Simple Pocket Fold

1. Keep the open edge of the leg on the side of the required foot. Crease fold on line indicated.

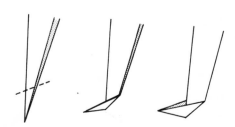
Figure 32. Foot — simple hood fold

2. Fold as shown forward and across. Straighten out leg.

3. Hold tip firmly and pull foot up between the open edges.

Foot – Double Pocket Fold

1. Crease fold on line indicated – note that the open edges are on the left although the foot will eventually go to the right.

2. Crease fold to the front and to the back. Straighten out.

3. Pull the tip through – as in the simple pocket fold.

4. Pull the foot under and back to the right-hand side – you will have made a double joint.

Figure 33.   Foot – simple pocket fold.

Figure 34.   Foot – double pocket fold

Head – Double Fold

1. Fold the head down as shown in the simple hood fold. Make additional crease folds on lines indicated.

2. Hood fold to form the head and crease and flatten folds for the beak.

3. Push first of beak folds into the head and bring the second of them out again.

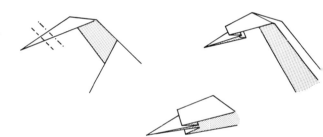

Figure 35.   Head – double fold

Head – Combined Hood and Pocket Folds

1. Make first crease fold at turn of the head. Note that the double but open edges of the model are on the side to which the head will go.

2. Crease fold both to the back and to the front.

3. Make pocket fold and an additional crease fold for the beak.

4. Crease fold both to the back and to the front.

5. Hood fold on crease line.

6. Pull out the under (single) edge to form this diamond. Double crease fold for the beak.

7. Push the first crease fold for the beak into the head and bring the second one out again. By adjusting the position of the crease, a great variety of expressions can be given to the various birds.

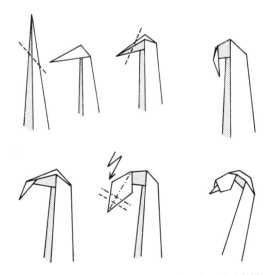

Figure 36.   Head – combined hood and pocket folds

24

CHAPTER 4

Simple Toys for Small Fingers

This chapter is virtually a collection of paper models used by generations of small children. Some of these you may have forgotten — others you may not have known. Included in this collection you will find:

An easy swan: For a model 4 × 2 you will need paper 7½ × 7½.

A tail plane: For a model 7 × 2½ (plus the length of the tail) you will need paper 8 × 8 for the body and 8 × 2 for the tail.

Parasol for a doll: The length of the 'fabric' section of the parasol is one half the diagonal of the square.

Jumping fox: For a model 2½ × 2½ use paper 7 × 7.

Flapping bird: Paper 8 × 8 makes a model 6 × 4.

Delta-wing plane: For a model 4 × 5 use a rectangle of paper 5 × 7.

Blow-up frog: For a model 3 × 4½ use paper 8 × 8.

Small dog: For a model 1½ × 2 use a square of paper 3 × 3.

Basket for small dog: To accommodate a 1½ × 2 dog use paper 7 × 7.

Boomerang: For a model 3 × 4 use a rectangle of paper 3½ × 7.

An easy house: For a model 6½ × 3¼ use a square of paper 6½ × 6½.

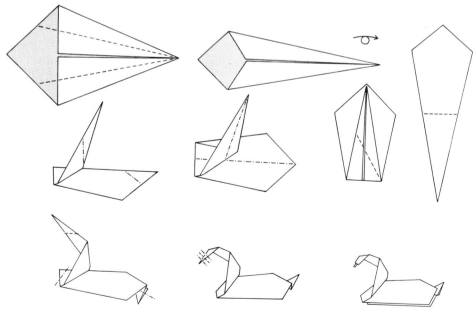

Figure 37. Swan

Easy Swan

Basic fold four.

1. Turn the model to the position shown in diagram 1. Crease fold on lines shown.
2. Fold upper and lower edges to centre.
3. Turn model to vertical position and crease fold on line shown.
4. Fold lower tip up to meet top. Crease fold on lines shown.
5. Half turn model to the right. Crease fold model in half keeping the coloured side of the paper to the outside. Fold top flap, on line made by earlier crease, up to form neck.
6. Fold model in half. Crease fold on lines shown for head and tail sections.
7. Pocket fold on creases and crease fold on lines shown.
8. Hood fold head section and pocket fold tail and breast section. Crease fold for beak.
9. Turn tip under and make a double fold for the beak.

Variations can be made by adjusting the length of the neck, by altering the position of the folds. Make a group of swans — some eating, some turning, some about to take to flight.

Paper $7\frac{1}{2} \times 7\frac{1}{2}$. Model 4×2.

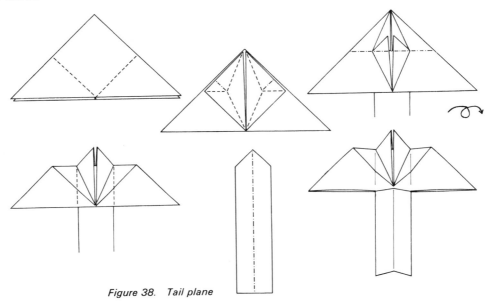

Figure 38.   Tail plane

Tail Plane

Basic fold three.

1. Turn basic fold to position shown. Crease fold top layer of side points on lines shown.
2. Fold and press firmly on previous crease lines. Crease on lines indicated — first folding the lower sides on the inner square to the centre and after pressing them firmly releasing them again and then the upper ones.
3. Fold in the sides of the square on previous crease folds allowing the centre to rise as shown. Crease fold to the back on lines indicated.
4. Fold top point over and down, turn model and make crease folds on wings as indicated, bringing the wings up a little.
5. Make a tail piece from a rectangle of paper the same length and one quarter the width of the main piece. Fold sides to centre and tuck in corners to make them fit into the nose piece of the plane. If necessary use glue to keep the pieces together.

When flying the planes a change of direction can be obtained by adjusting the wing or nose sections.

Paper 8×8 } Model $8 \times 2\frac{1}{2}$ (including
Paper 8×2 } tail).

Doll's Parasol

Basic fold six.

1. Keep basic fold in given position with the open ends to the top.
2. Fold upper flap from the left-hand side in to the centre. Crease fold and press flat. Open it out again.
3. Lift the flap again and apply gentle pressure to open and divide the paper. Press flat to achieve shape shown. Repeat the fold with other corners.
4. This model shows folding completed. A small Kebab or some such stick is then inserted (5).

Avoid sharp points if models are to be given to children. Small parasols are attractive when used for sandwich identification. Length of parasol is one half the diagonal of original square.

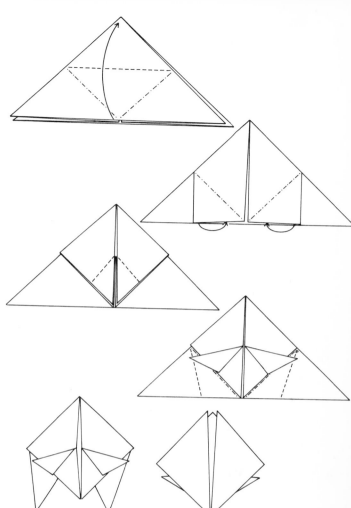

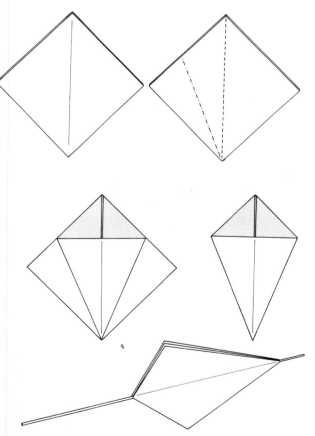

Figure 39.   Parasol

Figure 40.   Jumping fox

Jumping Fox

Basic fold three.

1. Turn basic fold to position shown. Crease fold on lines indicated. Lift centre point of crease taking it up to meet the top..
2. Finished fold looks like this. Crease and pocket fold corners.
3. Fold up the lower points on lines indicated to form the feet.
4. Pleat fold the sides taking first a fold to the back and then a fold forward on lines shown.
5. Finished fold will look like this. You have the fox which will, when his tail is tapped, jump for you.

Paper 7 × 7. Model $2\frac{1}{2}$ × $2\frac{1}{2}$.

Flapping Bird

Basic fold seven.

1. Bring basic fold to the position shown. Crease fold lower points to the back on lines indicated. Pocket fold on these crease lines.
2. Crease and pocket fold left-hand point for the head. Crease and fold the front wing forward and down.
3. The finished bird.
4. To make the bird flap its wings hold firmly between thumb and first finger at the spot marked by a circle and pull the tail section gently.

Paper 8 × 8. Model 6 × 4.

Figure 41. Flapping bird

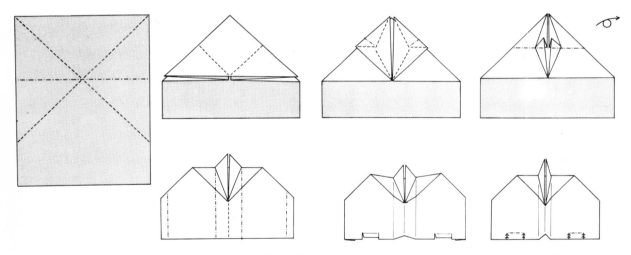

Figure 42. Delta-wing plane

Delta-wing Plane

Rectangle of paper.

1. Crease fold — the diagonal creases form a square — diagonally and horizontally.
2. Fold paper forward and down on the horizontal line. Fold sides in on crease folds as though you were making a Basic Fold Six. Crease fold top layers, right and left, forward and up to meet the top point.
3. Fold sides up to make a small inner square. Crease fold on lines shown, folding the lower edges to the centre and flattening out again. Crease fold the upper edges to the centre and flatten out again.
4. Fold the sides to the centre and in doing so allow the centre to rise as a point. Crease fold to the back along line indicated.
5. Turn model over. Crease along lines shown to shape the wings.
6. Cut and fold down 'flaps' on each wing.
7. Finished model.

Paper 5 × 7. Model 4 × 5.

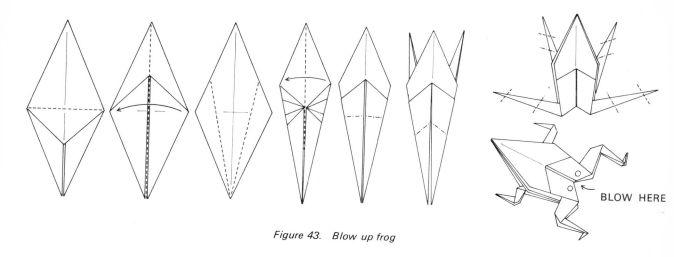

Figure 43. Blow up frog

Blow-up Frog

Basic fold eight.

1. Turn basic fold to the position shown. Crease fold on line shown.
2. Fold up small flaps – both front and back. Crease fold in half on line shown.
3. Fold top right flap to left and lower left to the right keeping four flaps on either side. Crease fold on lines shown taking sides forward to centre – repeat on each plain side.
4. Fold sides to centre. Crease fold model in half.
5. Fold top right side across to the left and bottom left side under to the right, keeping four flaps on each side. Crease fold on lines shown.
6. Fold the two under bottom flaps up on crease line to an almost vertical position. Crease fold on lines shown.
7. Pocket fold the remaining two lower flaps out to their respective sides. Crease fold on lines indicated.
8. Make two pocket folds on each leg. Hold on circle symbols and blow up the frog.
Paper 8 × 8. Model 3 × 4½.

Small Dog

Basic fold four.

1. Turn basic fold until it is in position shown. Fold the lower tip back and up to meet tip at the top. Turn model over so that double points are at the bottom.
2. Fold upper flap forward and up, making pleat as shown.
3. Starting at the bottom of the model and working upwards; fold lower point forward and up for tail section. Make a backward and then a forward fold to form head and ear.
4. Fold the top tip in and back for nose.
5. Fold the left- and right-hand corners of the top section in and back to shape the nose.
6. Fold the model in half by taking the left side back and across to the right.
7. Crease fold – front right flap forward and rear flap back. Pull the point out and back towards the head so that the head section is raised from the back.
8. Turn the model into a sitting position, pull up the tail a little and colour in a small section for the actual nose.

By using paper of different sizes a dog and puppies can be made to sit in the basket. White dogs can be given black spots – different coloured papers can also ring changes. A small cushion placed in the bottom of the basket finishes the set piece. These sets can be used for place names at a children's party – the name being printed on the side of the basket.
Paper 3 × 3. Model 1½ × 2.

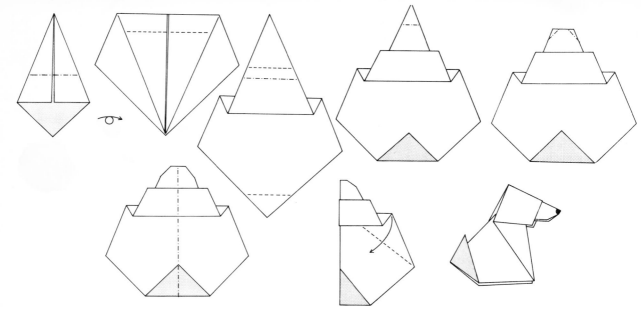

Figure 44. Dog

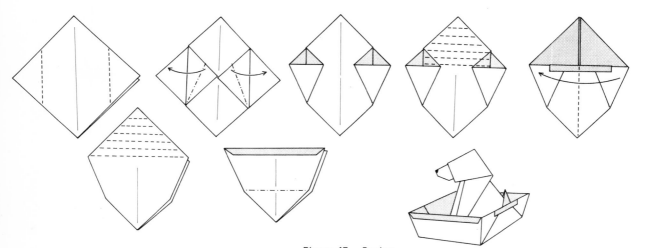

Figure 45. Basket

Basket — used as a bed for the dog
Basic fold six.

1. Turn the basic fold to position shown with the open points at the top. Crease fold both left- and right-hand corners, top flaps only, forward to meet in the centre.

2. Fold the points over and press firmly. Crease fold the centre points out again on lines shown.

3. Lift and flatten these points into arrow-like shapes. Turn the model over. Repeat on other side.

4. Having completed the arrow-like shapes on this side roll down the top layer of the open end and press firmly. Turn model over and repeat movement on other side.

5. With the folded ends of the basket now firmly secured bring the plain sides to the front and to the back by folding the top flap of the right-hand side over to the left and the

30

lower flap of the left-hand side under to the right.

6. Roll the top points down on lines shown. Crease fold, both to the back and to the front, the lower point.

7. This shows movement six completed.

8. Open out the model — note the usefulness of the crease fold in forming the square base. Paper 7 × 7. Model 4 × 4.

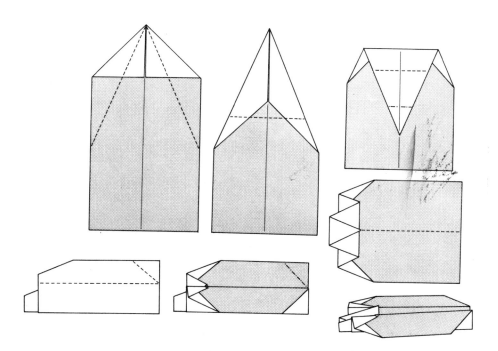

Figure 46. *Boomerang*

Boomerang

One half of a basic square (fold and divide square into two equal rectangles).

1. With right side of the paper uppermost, fold the two top corners in to meet in the centre. Crease fold from top central point down either side to enable the folded edges to meet in the centre.

2. Fold top edges down. Crease fold top point forward and down on line indicated.

3. Fold point down and crease fold on lines indicated, judging the distances carefully.

4. Half turn the model to the right. Crease fold model in half.

5. Fold model in half by taking lower edge forward and up to meet top edge. Crease fold on lines indicated, taking the tail crease forward and down and then the wing down to the lower edge.

6. Repeat the folds on the other wing.

7. Boomerang ready for use.

Paper $3\frac{1}{2}$ × 7. Model 3 × 4.

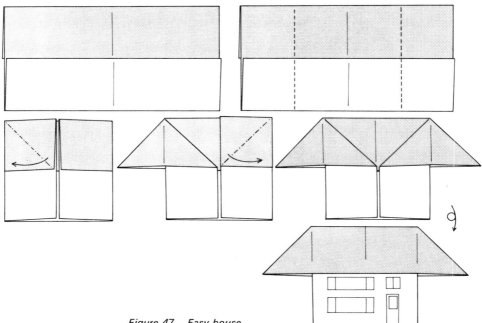

Figure 47. Easy house

Easy House

1. With the right side of the paper towards you, fold the lower quarter of the sheet forward and up and the upper quarter back and down.

2. Crease fold the left- and right-hand sides forward to meet in the middle.

3. Fold the sides in and crease fold the inner top corners back and down on line shown.

4. Bring the inner top corners down and by applying slight pressure flatten them to form the eaves of the house.

5. Back of house.

6. Turn model over and draw in windows, doors and such like.

Paper $6\frac{1}{2} \times 6\frac{1}{2}$. Model $6\frac{1}{2} \times 3\frac{1}{4}$.

CHAPTER 5

Easter Scene

Base: Make a base from a selection of squares of assorted sizes made in varying shades of green. A better base is made if you open and interlock these. Instructions are given for doing this. Glue the intersecting flaps in place and mount the completed base on a sheet of stiff board.

It is possible to hold both the cockerel and the hen in a standing position by tucking their feet under one of the cross folds of the base. Cut small pieces of green tissue paper into tufts of grass and tuck a small section of each under a fold to keep it in position. The small chicks, charming when made in yellow tissue paper, need no support when placed on the base, but if you wish to use them as a decoration for eggs or napkin rings use a small blob of egg white or glue to hold them. The models for the Easter Scene were made from paper of the following sizes :

Hen: $8\frac{1}{2} \times 8\frac{1}{2}$.

Cock (compound) : Head section $9\frac{1}{2} \times 9\frac{1}{2}$. Tail section $9\frac{1}{2} \times 9\frac{1}{2}$.

Chicks: $2\frac{1}{2} \times 2\frac{1}{2}$ for each.

Grass: $1 \times \frac{1}{2}$.

Box: to hold small Easter eggs. 8×8.

Figure 48. Easter Scene

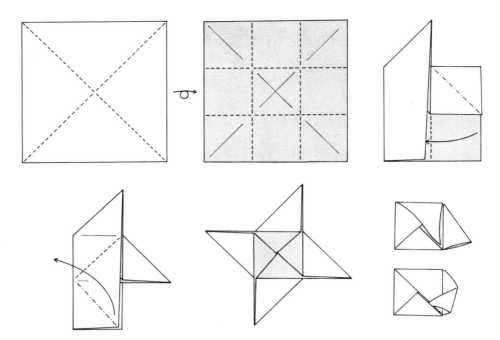

Figure 49. Basic shape for screens, bases and cushions

Basic Shape for Screens, Bases and Cushions

1. Crease fold paper into triangles and open out again.
2. Crease fold into ninths, and open out again.
3. Fold top and left sections in, leaving original top left point extending.
4. Fold in right side along crease folds previously made — leaving original right top point extended.
5. Fold in lower edge so that the remaining two original corners extend, thus making a windmill.
6. In clockwise order fold the extensions in towards the centre, one overlapping the other.
7. Tuck the last flap in, thus securing the others.
Paper 9 × 9 makes base 3 × 3.

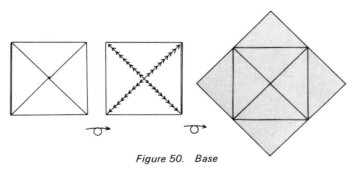

Figure 50. Base

Base for Easter Scene

1. Basic shape.
2. Turn model over and cut top layer of paper along the lines shown. Start at the centre and cut towards each corner. Open out the cut flaps.
3. Turn the model over and utilise as many of the flaps as you require for intersecting one into another to form a screen or a base.

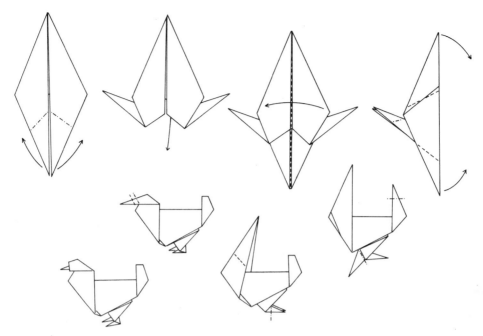

Figure 51. Hen

Hen

Basic fold seven.

1. Turn basic fold to position shown. Crease fold on lines indicated.
2. Pocket fold the lower points out to their respective sides.
3. Bring the rear flap down and fold model in half by bringing the right-hand side forward and across to meet the left.
4. Crease fold firmly on lines shown.
5. Turn the model and make a hood fold, using previous crease folds on the right for the tail and on the left for the head. Pocket fold the feet in the direction of the tail. Fold down the tip of the tail.
6. Crease fold for the head and feet.
7. Bring the crease fold for the head into a hood; fold and crease fold on lines shown for the beak. Pocket fold the feet in the direction of the head.
8. Make double fold for the beak.

Pull out the folds slightly to give the hen a little plumpness. If you intend to use this hen as part of the Easter Scene, we suggest that you use brown paper for it and yellow tissue paper for the chicks.
Paper $8\frac{1}{2} \times 8\frac{1}{2}$. Model 4×4.

Cockerel – Head Section

Basic fold seven.

1. Turn basic fold to position shown. Crease fold on lines indicated.
2. Fold model in half by bringing the right-hand side forward to meet the left.
3. Hood fold on lines previously creased. Crease fold on line shown.
4. Pocket fold both flaps of head section down.
5. Pocket fold inner flap of head section up. Crease fold on lines shown – twice for wings, twice on beak and twice on comb.
6. Pleat fold on wing creases, double pocket fold for comb and beak.

Paper $9\frac{1}{2} \times 9\frac{1}{2}$.

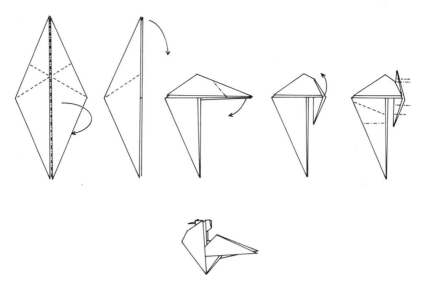

Figure 52. Cockerel – head section

Cockerel – Rear Section
Basic fold seven.

1. Turn basic fold to position shown. Crease fold on lines indicated.

2. Pocket fold the lower points out to their respective sides. Crease fold these points in half taking the folds to the inside.

3. Fold on previous crease lines and press firmly. Crease fold top flaps down – one to the back and one to the front on lines shown.

4. Fold the flaps down and crease fold model in half by bringing the right forward and over to the left-hand side.

5. Make the fold and press firmly. Crease

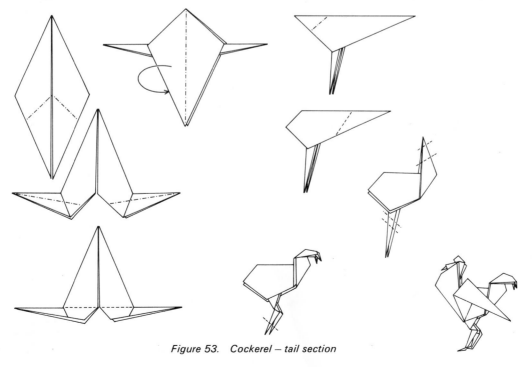

Figure 53. Cockerel – tail section

fold the body on lines shown — both to the front and to the back.

6. Pocket fold the left-hand point — this is then ready to insert into the head section.

7. Hood fold the tail up and make the crease folds on tail and legs in positions shown.

8. Hood and then pocket fold the tail section. Double pocket fold for the leg joints and hood fold for the feet.

To complete the model insert the rear into the head section and glue in position.

9. Shows the completed model.

Paper for rear section $9\frac{1}{2} \times 9\frac{1}{2}$.

Paper for head section $9\frac{1}{2} \times 9\frac{1}{2}$.

Completed model $6 \times 4\frac{3}{4}$.

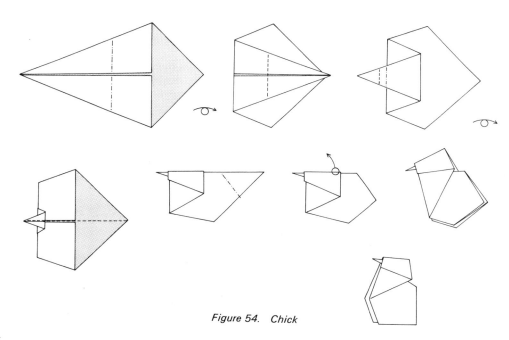

Figure 54. Chick

Chick

Basic fold four.

1. Turn the basic fold to the position shown.

2. Fold the left point backward and over to a point just beyond that on the right. Turn model over.

3. Fold the tip back over to the left again. Keep this fold in line with the upper and lower points. Crease fold on lines shown.

4. Turn the model over and double fold the tip in the manner shown.

5. Fold the model in half by bringing the top forward and down over the bottom half.

6. Fold in the right-hand point to shape the rear end.

7. Give shape to the model by pulling the head section up and out until the head is above the body. Pull down the beak a little. Turn the model into a sitting position.

In this simple model symbols have been kept to an absolute minimum to give you an alternative approach to folding.

Paper $2\frac{1}{2} \times 2\frac{1}{2}$. Model $1 \times 1\frac{1}{2}$.

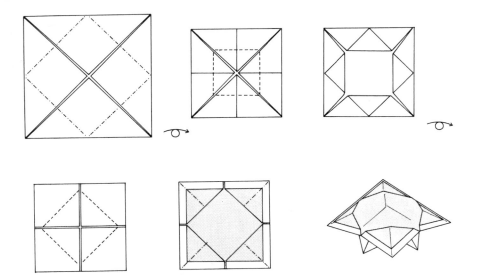

Figure 55. Box

Box — a particularly pretty and useful model
Basic fold five.

1. Bring basic fold to position shown and crease fold.

2. Turn basic shape over and fold corners to the centre. Crease fold inner points on lines shown.

3. Fold corners to the outer edges to form a base. Turn the model over.

4. Fold centre points out towards corners — leaving a little band as a decoration.

5. Crease fold the top on lines shown.

6. Open up the box by lifting the corners and pressing down the base (on inner square).

Paper 8 × 8. Model 2 × 2.

CHAPTER 6

Roundabout

This makes a delightful table decoration or plaything and requires:

A metal rod or knitting needle 6 in. long.

A substantial cork or a small wooden block to support the roundabout rod.

A piece of stiff paper or thin card from which it is possible to cut a circle 9 in. in diameter. This is used as a platform for the models.

A piece of stiff paper or thin card from which it is possible to cut 7 supports — each one being 4 in. long and $\frac{1}{2}$ in. wide.

A piece of stiff paper or thin card from which it is possible to cut a circle 5 in. in diameter.

For the decorative roof of the roundabout you will need two squares in different colours from which you will be able to cut strips 3 in. wide. These will be pleated and placed alternately on the firm roof disc to form a sort of decorative umbrella. You will need a total of about 22 in. in length.

A short thread with which to fasten the top of the pleats.

For the animals, we have chosen to use:

Swan: paper $8\frac{1}{2} \times 8\frac{1}{2}$; model $5 \times 3\frac{1}{2}$.

Pig: paper $4\frac{1}{2} \times 4\frac{1}{2}$; model $3 \times 1\frac{1}{2}$.

Fish: paper 5×5; model $6 \times 1\frac{1}{2}$.

Duck: paper 3×3; model 2×1.

Duck — simple fold: paper $4\frac{1}{2} \times 4\frac{1}{2}$; model $3 \times 2\frac{1}{2}$.

Snapper: paper 6×6; model 3×3.

When substituting other animals try to use paper of similar size, and then you will have no difficulty with the balance of the roundabout.

Figure 56. Roundabout

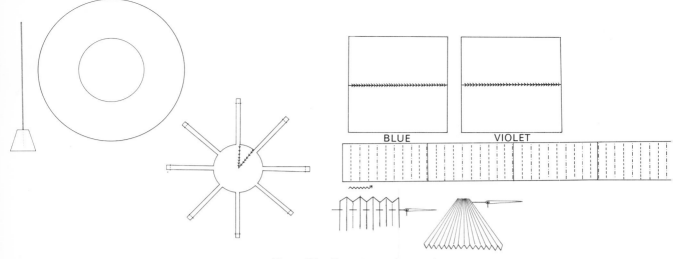

Figure 57. Base, top and supports

Base, Top and Supports

1. Cut one circle 9 in. in diameter. From the centre of this cut out a smaller circle 3¾ in. in diameter.

2. From the smaller piece of stiff paper cut a circle 5 in. in diameter and mark it into eighths. Cut out one of the segments, and close the gap. The effect of this will be to make a shallow cone. At each of the remaining points glue a support into position. The supports, ½ in. wide and 4 in. long will also need to be made from stiff paper. Then glue supports to large circle base.

3. Make pleated top to decorate roof of roundabout from four alternate half square strips of blue and violet paper.

4. & 5. Baste top of pleated strip with needle and thread. Draw together as shown.

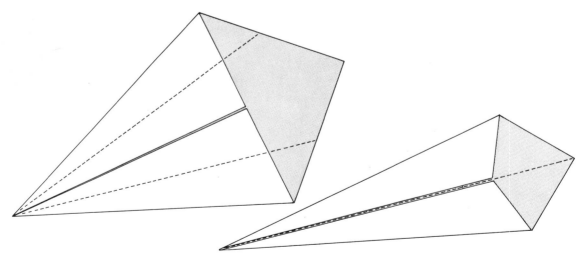

Figure 58(a)   Swan

Swan

Basic fold four.

1. Turn fold to position shown. Crease fold on lines indicated.

2. Fold in top and bottom edges to the centre. Crease fold model in half by taking the top side forward and down over the lower one.

40

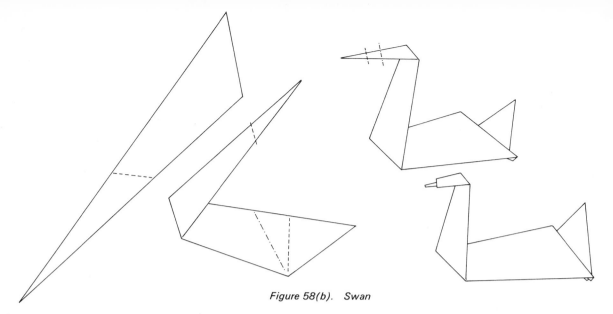

Figure 58(b). Swan

3. Fold model in half. Crease fold on line shown to form neck.
4. Make hood fold on crease line. Crease fold on lines shown.
5. Hood fold for head section. Double pocket fold for tail. Crease fold on lines shown for beak.
6. Make double pocket fold for beak and your simple swan is complete.
Paper $8\frac{1}{2} \times 8\frac{1}{2}$. Model $5 \times 3\frac{1}{2}$.

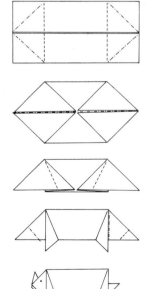

Pig
Basic fold one.
1. Make basic fold and open out. Fold top and bottom edges to centre line. Make crease folds on lines indicated taking the diagonal ones to the back and the vertical ones to the front.
2. Bring each corner up and flatten it out so that it falls into a triangle as shown.
3. Fold model in half by taking the lower section up and behind the upper one thus bringing the open ends to the bottom. Crease fold inner flaps of the triangles forward and out. Repeat on the other side.
4. Fold sections of the triangles, on previous crease folds, forward to form the legs. Make a crease fold for the nose and two for the tail section on the lines shown.
5. Complete the animal by making a pocket fold for the snout and a double pocket fold for the tail section.
6. The nose can be varied by changing the type of fold. A small black dot for the eye helps to give the face expression.
Paper $4\frac{1}{2} \times 4\frac{1}{2}$. Model $3 \times 1\frac{1}{2}$.

Figure 59. Pig

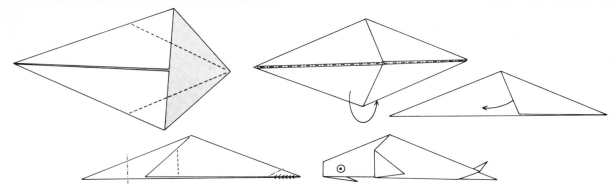

Figure 60. Fish

Fish
Basic fold four.

1. Turn to position shown and crease fold upper and lower edges on lines indicated.
2. Fold in on crease lines. Crease fold model in half by taking the top section to the back and down to meet the lower one.
3. Fold model in half. Turn so that the level edge is at the bottom.
4. Bring out the inner flaps to form fins and crease fold on line shown.
5. Pocket fold in for snout. Cut tail section on line indicated and turn one half of it up. Fold the fin back on crease fold and add an eye.

Paper 5 × 5. Model 6 × 1½.

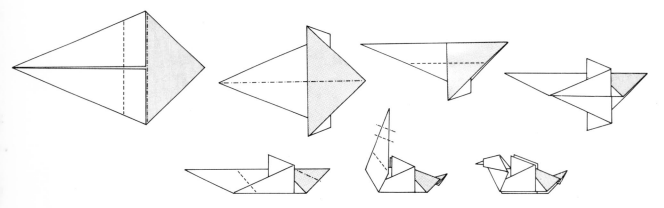

Figure 61. Duck

Duck
Basic fold four.

1. Turn the basic fold until it is in the position shown and crease fold.
2. Turn it over and bring the right-hand point over towards the left and flatten. Fold the single top flap back towards the right along the crease line shown. Crease fold model in half.
3. Fold the model in half by bringing the top section down behind the lower section. Crease fold the lower top flap forward and up, and the lower back flap back and up.
4. Fold on the crease lines already made — first the front flap and then the back one — and flatten.
5. Crease fold to both front and back on lines shown.
6. Hood fold crease at left point to form breast of bird. Pocket fold crease on right to form tail and pull out the tip. Crease fold on lines shown.
7. Make first a hood fold to form head and then a double pocket fold for beak.

Paper 3 × 3. Model 2 × 1.

Duck — simple fold

Basic fold four.

1. Place basic fold in horizontal position and crease fold top and bottom points forward to the centre line.

2. Fold and flatten on crease lines already made and crease along horizontal centre.

3. Fold in half by bringing lower point forward and up.

4. Turn model so that the open ends are pointing downwards. Crease fold on lines shown to form head and tail, creasing both to the back and to the front. Fold body section under into centre.

5. Hood fold for tail and neck and crease fold, both forwards and backwards, for head.

6. Make hood fold for head and double pocket fold for beak along crease folds already made. Add spot for eye.

This is a well-balanced model suitable for a mobile.

Paper $4\frac{1}{2} \times 4\frac{1}{2}$. Model $3 \times 2\frac{1}{2}$.

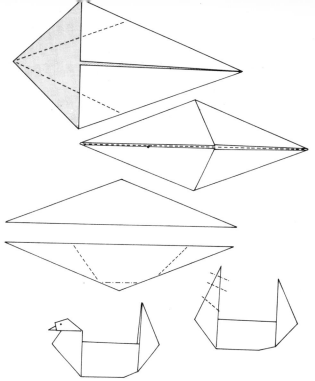

Figure 62. Duck — simple fold

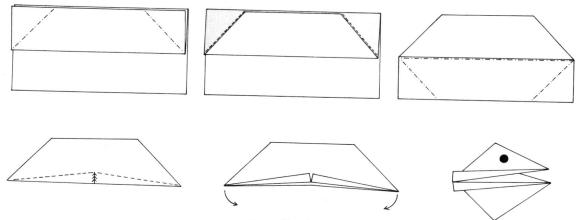

Figure 63. Snapper

Snapper

Basic square.

1. With the coloured side of the paper towards you, fold it in half by bringing the top down to meet the bottom. Fold the top layer in half again. Crease and fold the top left- and right-hand corners, top layer only, to the back.

2. Fold the left- and right-hand corners forward and in.

3. Fold the corners remaining back and in on lines shown. Fold the model in half, keeping the coloured side of the paper to the outside.

4. Make a small cut in the centre of the open

side where indicated. Crease fold edges to the outside.

5. Bring the snapper into use by pressing the ends down towards each other as directed by the arrows. A small patch can be added for the eye. When not in use the snapper remains flat.

6. Finished model.

Paper 6 × 6. Model 3 × 3.

7. Glue an eye onto each side and, using just a drop of clear, quick drying glue, fix all to the roundabout base. Keep the snapper's beak open by passing a thread through as shown, and fastening with knots.

Figure 64. Gluing

CHAPTER 7

The Ark

By combining a house and a boat and adding a gangway we have an ark. Make your own selection of animals to go with it. In this chapter we have included a variety of models, but suggest that you use others from different parts of the book. Animals and birds which do not appear elsewhere and which could be included in a scene featuring an ark are:

Mouse
Snake
Snail
Elephant
Camel
Peacock
Small Bird

In addition to the animals and birds you will need :
House made from two sheets of paper, each 17 × 17 (Model 17 × 8½).
Boat made from one sheet of paper 26 × 21 (model 21 × 5).
Gangway from a rectangle of paper 17 × 5.

The size of the ark will of course be governed by the size of the animals, birds, etc. that you wish to stand near it. Normally, boats and houses made from simple folds are only fractionally shorter than the longest side of the rectangular paper from which they are made. The trees are made from paper 8 × 8 and will be 6½ inches high. The layered tree has been included as an alternative.

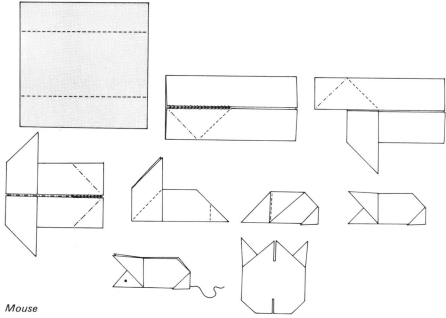

Figure 65.   Mouse

Mouse

Basic fold one.

1. Crease fold as shown.
2. Fold top and bottom edges in to meet this line. Crease fold on lines shown. Fold creases over to ascertain length of cut required. Release the fold and cut along line shown.
3. Lift the creased corners and with gentle pressure guide them into positions shown.
4. Folds completed. Crease fold on right-hand corners. Cut along line indicated. Crease fold model in half, keeping coloured side on the outside.
5. Pocket fold ends. Crease fold on lines shown.
6. Fold right- and left-hand ends towards the centre, both back and front. Crease fold on lines shown.
7. Fold flaps forward for ears.
8. Add spot for eye and a string for the tail.
9. This animal, when opened out, can be used as an invitation card.

Paper $5\frac{1}{2} \times 5\frac{1}{2}$. Model $3\frac{1}{2} \times 2\frac{1}{2}$.

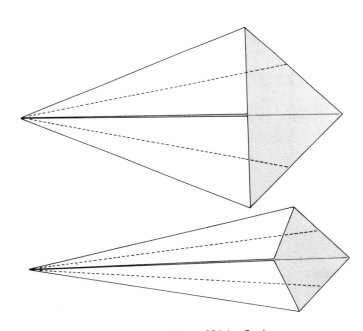

Figure 66(a). Snake

Snake

Basic fold four.

1. Turn fold so that the narrow point is to the left and crease fold long sides to centre.
2. Fold on lines shown, and then crease long sides again to centre.
3. Fold model in half by bringing upper section forward and down.
4. Crease fold and press on line shown, one quarter length from the end.

46

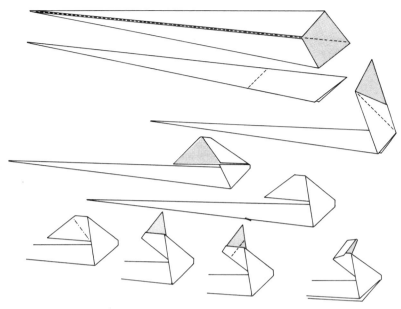

Figure 66(b).

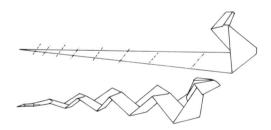

Figure 66(c).

5. Hood fold on crease and turn the model so that the open fold is at the bottom. Crease fold on line shown.
6. Bring crease fold forward and flatten.
7. Bring crease fold into pocket fold for head.
8. Crease fold the head flap to the back as indicated.
9. Bring it back and make pocket fold.
10. Crease fold forward on lines shown.
11. Using these lines make hood fold to bring head into striking position.
12. Crease fold along body decreasing the distance between the folds as the tail is reached.
13. Complete the snake by making alternate hood and pocket folds along the body. Bring down one side of the head fold to give the model character.

Paper $8\frac{1}{2} \times 8\frac{1}{2}$. Model $7 \times 1\frac{1}{2}$.

47

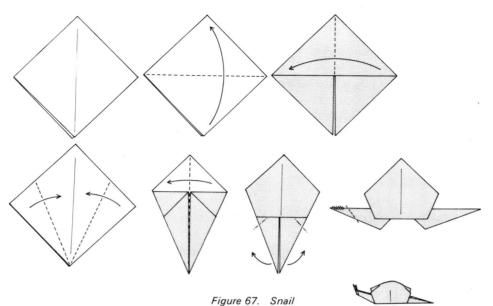

Figure 67. Snail

Snail

Basic fold six.

1. Turn basic fold to position shown.
2. Crease and fold the top layer of paper forward and up. Turn model over and repeat.
3. Fold the top right flap over to the left and the lower left flap under to the right.
4. Crease and fold the sides of the top layers to the centre on lines shown. Turn the model and repeat folds on the other side.

5. Folds completed.
6. Turn top layer of right-hand flaps over to the left and lower layer of left-hand flaps under to the right. Pocket fold the lower points out to their respective sides as shown.
7. Crease fold and cut for horns on lines indicated.
8. Flatten the model slightly to give it a little plumpness. Paper 6 × 6. Model 1½ × 2½.

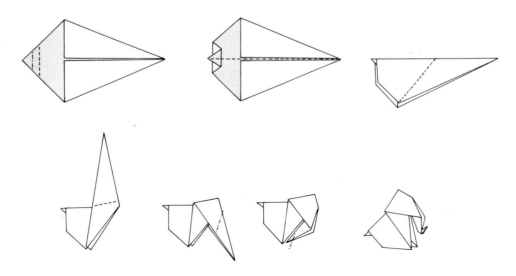

Figure 68. Elephant

Elephant

Basic fold four.
1. Bring basic fold in position shown.
2. Crease and fold in left-hand tip as shown.
3. Fold model in half. Crease fold on lines shown.
4. Make first hood fold and crease on lines shown.
5. Make a second hood fold and crease as shown.
6. Make a pocket fold on crease 3.
7. Turn model to standing position and pocket fold tip of trunk.
Paper 5 × 5. Model 3 × 3.

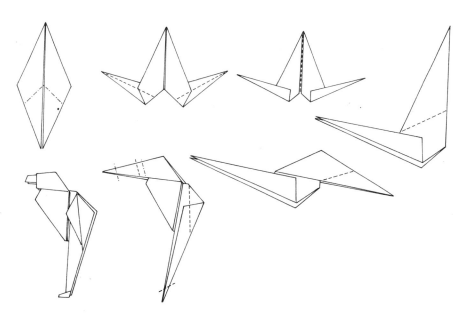

Figure 69. Camel – head section

Camel – Head Section

Basic fold seven.
1. Turn the basic fold to the position shown. Crease fold on lines indicated.
2. Pocket fold lower flaps to their respective sides taking them to a position above the horizontal. Crease fold flaps on lines shown taking the front ones forward and back ones to the rear.
3. Fold flaps on crease lines. Fold model in half by bringing right-hand side forward and over to the right.
4. Crease and make a hood fold on line shown.
5. Crease and hood fold again.
6. Turn model. Hood fold for head on crease fold made previously. Crease fold for shoulder head and feet on lines indicated.
7. Fold the shoulder sections in the direction of the head. Hood fold feet. Hood and pocket fold head and fold in the nose at a slight angle as indicated.
Paper 10 × 10. Model 6 × 6.

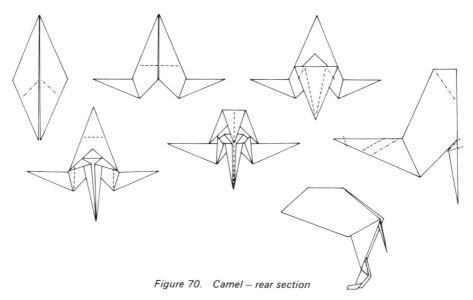

Figure 70. Camel – rear section

Camel – Rear Section

Basic fold seven.

1. Turn basic fold to position shown. Crease fold on lines indicated.

2. Pocket fold bottom points to side, keeping the tops of the folds horizontal. Crease fold top point on line shown.

3. Fold top flap down and crease fold sides to centre.

4. Fold sides to centre on crease folds, flattening the tops to form arrowheads as shown. Crease fold upper point and central flaps on lines shown.

5. Fold centre creases forward and top point down.

6. Fold model in half by taking the right-hand side forward and over to meet the left-hand side. This will form the body. Make firm crease folds where indicated.

7. Half turn the model to the right. Make a pocket fold to bring down the tail and a double pocket fold for the leg joints. For the feet a hood fold is needed and for the hooves a small pocket fold. Now turn your attention to forming the hump on the back. Do this by pushing down the folds lightly and flattening.

Complete the animal by joining the two parts together by inserting the rear into the head section – adjust the line and glue into position.

Paper for rear section 10 × 10.
Paper for head section 10 × 10.
Model 6 × 6.

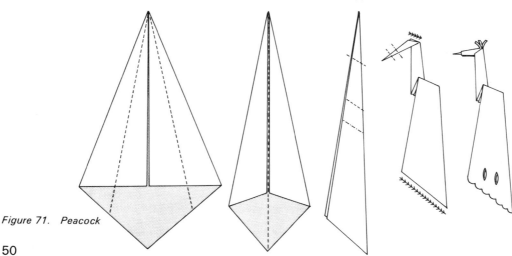

Figure 71. Peacock

Peacock
Basic fold four.
1. Turn basic fold to position shown. Crease fold on lines indicated.
2. Fold sides to centre. Crease fold model in half.
3. Fold model in half by taking the right side forward and over to the left. Crease fold on lines indicated.
4. Fold as shown. Crease fold for beak section and cut along the back edge of head fold.
5. Make a double pocket fold for the head and another for the beak. Cut a few strands of paper for the crest. Make a pattern at the base to represent the tail.

   The finished bird will be about three-quarters the diagonal measurement of the original square. It can be perched on the roof of the ark, or used to decorate an invitation card.

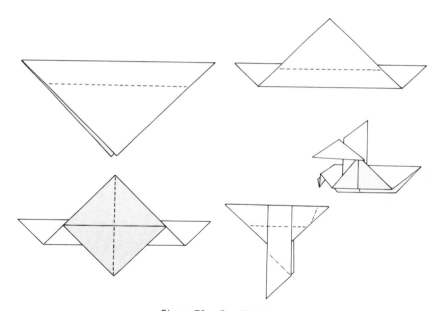

Figure 72. Small bird

Small Bird
Basic fold two.
1. Turn the basic fold to position shown. Crease fold on line indicated.
2. Fold both of the top points forward and up along the crease line.
3. Fold the front flap down just below the other line. Crease fold the model in half by bringing the right side forward to meet the left. Turn model to position shown and crease fold.
4. Fold the wings up on the line shown — one to the back and one to the front. Make a pocket fold for the beak and add movement by folding down a wing.
5. Completed Bird.
Paper 8 × 8. Model 6 × 4.

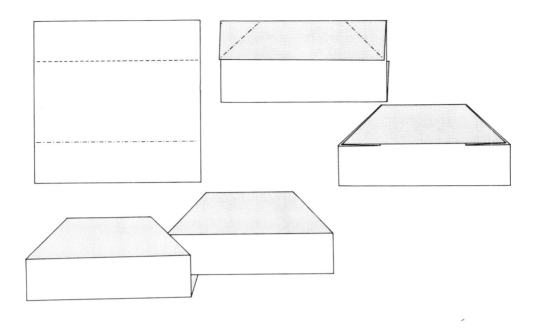

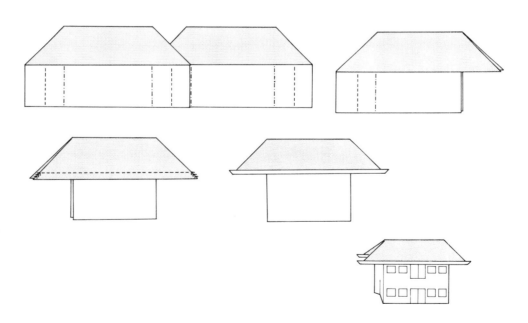

Figure 73.   House

House for the Ark

Two squares of paper 17 × 17.

1. Crease fold the lower quarter of the paper under and the upper quarter forward.
2. Fold the paper. Crease the two top corners on lines shown.
3. Pocket fold both of these corners down and in. Repeat with second sheet of paper.
4. Overlap the two ends and fasten with a little glue bringing each end into line with the corner of the roof. Do not fasten the roof sections together.
5. Crease fold to the back and to the front as indicated.
6. Fold in the centre creases and release the eaves. Complete the other end of the house.
7. Cut a small section of the eaves to enable the gutters to be formed. Crease fold.
8. Fold up the edges to form the gutters.
9. Decorate in manner suitable for an ark. Join front and back section of the roof with a little glue.

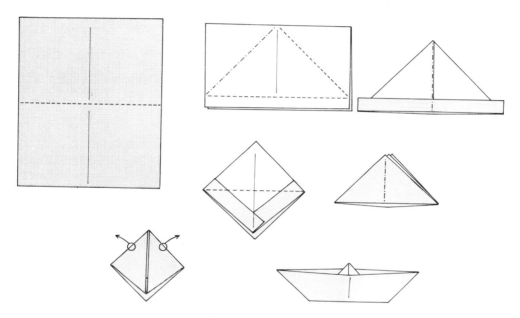

Figure 74. Boat

Boat for the Ark

Rectangle of paper.

1. Crease fold in half as shown, with wrong side of paper uppermost.
2. Fold paper in half, bringing the coloured side to the outside. Crease fold on lines shown, taking the left-hand corner to the back and the right-hand one to the front. Crease fold the lower edges up and out.
3. Make folds. Crease fold model in half.
4. Fold model in half by pressing the outer corners in towards each other. Crease fold to the back and to the front on line indicated.
5. Fold model in half, taking the front section forward and up and the back section to the back and up. Crease fold to the back and to the front on line indicated.
6. Fold model in half by pressing outer edges in towards each other.
7. Exerting a little pressure, separate the two points. Lift them and pull the model more or less inside out.

You will have realised when making this model that you have in fact made at least three model hats. This boat, combined with the house, makes the ark.

Paper 26 × 21. Model 21 × 5.

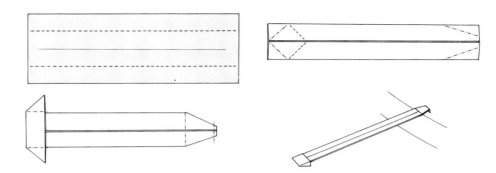

Figure 75.   Gangway

Gangway for the Ark
Rectangle of paper.
1. Crease fold long edges to the centre.
2. Fold in the edges. Crease fold ends on lines indicated.

3. Fold left-hand end forward and over. Fold sides of the right-hand end under and back. Crease fold to the back on lines shown.
4. Gangway shown in position.
Paper 17 × 5. Model $2\frac{1}{2}$ × 15.

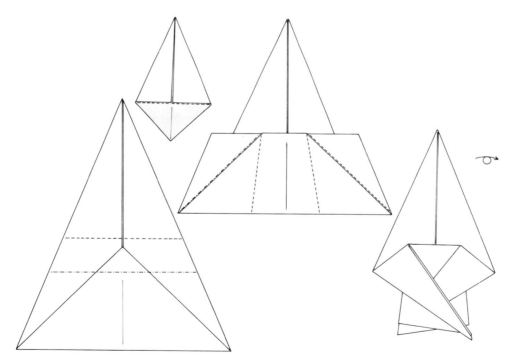

Figure 76.   Easy tree

Easy Tree
Basic fold four.
1. Place basic fold in position shown – with

narrow point at the top and crease and fold lower point up on line indicated.
2. Make two folds on lines shown.

3. Crease fold the top layer of the model along the lines indicated — by bringing the outer points in towards and past the centre of the model and pressing along the line to make the fold flat. You will note that the 'trunk' of the tree is wider at the base.

4. Complete the folds and flatten. Note the projecting roots of the trees.

5. Turn the model over and crease fold to make a firm base. Tuck the ends in along the crease line.

6. Push into shape a little.

Paper 8 × 8. Height of Model 6½ in.

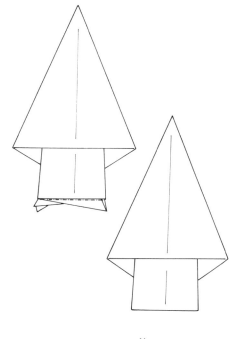

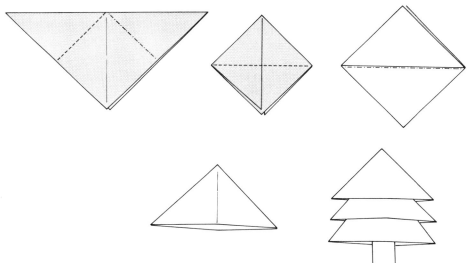

Figure 77. Layered tree

Layered Tree

This tree can be used with or without a trunk. Basic fold two, with the plain side of the paper on the outside.

1. Turn basic fold to position shown. Crease fold on lines indicated, taking the right-hand corner to the back and the left-hand corner to the front.

2. Make folds. Crease fold on line indicated.

3. Divide the flaps, taking the front section forward and up and the remainder to the back and up.

4. Make three or four of these models, and place them one above the other.

Each section is one eighth the size of the original paper. Use a roll of paper for the trunk.

CHAPTER 8

Hospital Room or Room for a Doll's House

To make this group to scale, you will need :

Room: a rectangle of heavy paper or light card $30\frac{1}{2} \times 19$.

Nurse: a square 7×7 for her gown, and a smaller square in white, 3×3, for her head-dress.

Bed: thick paper $8\frac{3}{4} \times 10\frac{3}{4}$.

Carpet: 6 squares in different colours each $3\frac{1}{2} \times 3\frac{1}{2}$.

Nest of tables: squares, varying from 4×4 to $2\frac{1}{4} \times 2\frac{1}{4}$.

Plant container: paper $3\frac{1}{2} \times 3\frac{1}{2}$.

Plant: divide a $3\frac{1}{2} \times 3\frac{1}{2}$ square into four and use one section for one leaf.

To make a dining room, use a dining table and chairs instead of the bed. You will need :

Dining table: paper $8\frac{1}{2} \times 8\frac{1}{2}$.

Chairs: paper $8\frac{1}{2} \times 4\frac{1}{2}$ for each.

Cushions: squares of paper, 3×3.

Figure 78. Hospital Scene

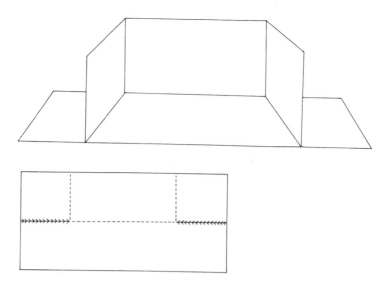

Figure 79. Room

Room
Use a rectangle of stiff card $30\frac{1}{2} \times 19$.
1. Mark it in half lengthwise and then the rear section into quarters. Cut cleanly along one quarter from the left and one quarter from the right.
2. Fold up the back section of the card and bring in the cut sides to form walls.

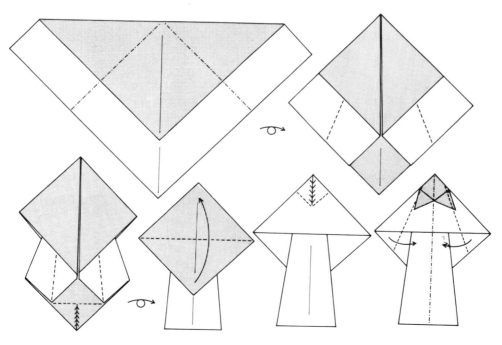

Figure 80. Nurse

Nurse

Use a square of paper with wrong side towards you to make body.

1. Fold down the top section of the square as shown. Crease fold on lines indicated.

2. Turn paper over and fold left- and right-hand points to the centre. Crease fold on lines shown.

3. Fold lines to the back. Crease fold again on lines shown. Cut and crease fold lower point forward.

4. Turn model over and crease fold on line shown.

5. Fold up top flap. Cut along line indicated. Crease fold cut points forward and down.

6. Shape the model by crease folding it in half to the back. Fold the top points down and crease and fold the sides in over them. If desired, decorate with a cross.

7. From a smaller square of paper, crease fold a rectangle five-eighths of its width.

8. Cut along the line indicated.

9. Fold extra eighth forward and down.

10. Crease fold sides to near centre.

11. Fold in on crease lines. Crease fold sides to centre again.

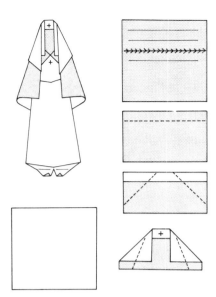

12. Fold in sides. Add second cross if desired and put the headdress on the model. A small back holder may be necessary to keep the model in a standing position.

Paper 7 × 7 for body.

Paper 3½ × 3½ for headdress.

Finished model 5 inches high.

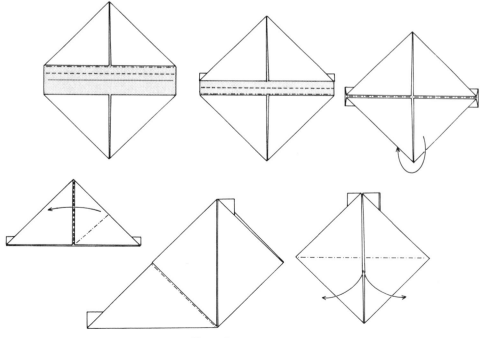

Figure 81. Bed

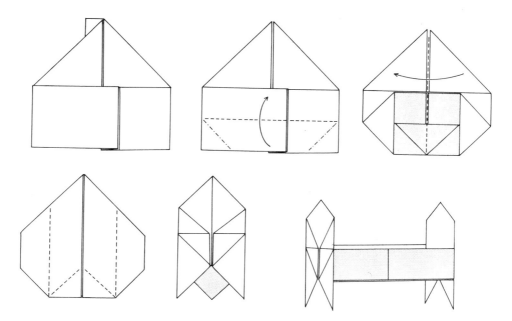

Bed

You will need stiff paper — use a rectangle.

1. Fold the four corners of the rectangle forward and down to the centre. Crease fold centre section on lines shown.

2. Fold the top section down and the bottom section up on lines indicated.

3. Crease fold model in half.

4. Fold model in half. Crease fold right-hand section both forward and back. Lift the right-hand point over towards the centre and flatten it to form a diamond.

5. Turn the model over and repeat the move. This brings one set of pleats to the front and one to the back. Crease fold front flap on line shown.

6. Fold front flap down but when doing so open out the single folds of paper to form a rectangle as shown, (7).

8. Crease fold the lower rectangle in half.

9. Lift the centre pleated layer up to the top of the rectangle. Flatten the ends to form triangles. Turn the model over and repeat on the other side. Change the model to form ends by taking the top right-hand flap forward and over to the left, and the lower left-hand flap under and over to the right.

10. Crease fold on lines shown.

11. Fold lower points forward and up and then side edges in to meet in the centre.

12. Pull the ends of the bed apart gently allowing the concertina folds to straighten out.

This model is also used for the sleigh in the Christmas scene.

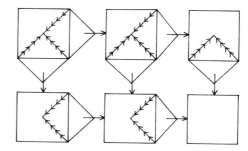

Figure 82. Carpet

Carpet

1. From different coloured papers make six squares, following the instructions given for the base of the Easter set.

2. Turn the bases over and cut along lines indicated. Intersect the bases and glue into position.

Paper $3\frac{1}{2} \times 3\frac{1}{2}$. Individual square approx. 1. Size of finished mat made from six such squares $3\frac{1}{2} \times 2\frac{1}{2}$.

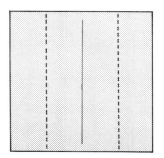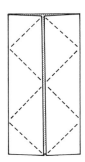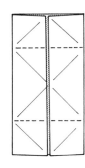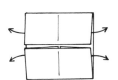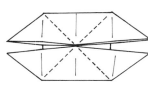

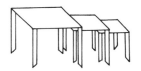

Figure 83.   Nest of tables

Nest of Tables

Basic square.

1. Fold two sides to centre.
2. Crease fold along lines indicated — flatten.
3. Fold short sides to centre.
4. Lift flaps to enable you to take original corners out to the side. Repeat with other points. These will form the legs.
5. Bring points to upright position to form four legs. Reverse model and stand.

6. Finished model, standing.

Nest of tables for dolls' house — alternative legs:

7. Turn the tables upside down and cut along lines shown. Stiffer paper will be needed for these slender-legged nests of tables.
8. Finished tables.

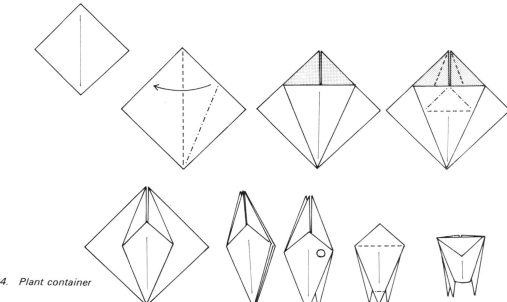

Figure 84.   Plant container

Plant Container

The basic folding for this takes you through from Basic Fold Six to Basic Fold Eight. Try to follow it through without the written instruction.

1. Basic Fold Six — open ends at the top.
2. Crease fold on lines shown, creasing only the top flap on the right-hand side.
3. Lift the crease fold and flatten it as indicated.
4. Fold in inner top flaps.
5. Lift centre to allow the sides to fold under it.
6. Repeat with the remaining three flaps.
7. Hold where indicated, and pocket fold the upper points down one by one.
8. Crease fold on lines shown.
9. Fold top flaps down — one to the back and one to the front. Square off the base and open out the model.

Paper 4 × 4. Model 1½ × 1.

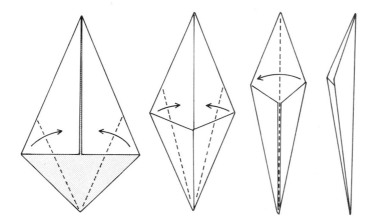

Figure 85. Plant

Plant

Use a square of paper 3 × 3, and divide it into quarters — this will make four leaves.
For one leaf — basic fold four.

1. Turn basic fold to position shown. Crease fold on lines indicated.
2. Fold lower edges in to the centre.

Crease fold on lines shown.

3. Fold lower sides to centre. Crease fold model in half by taking the right side forward and over to meet the left. Curl the leaves and make secure with a little blob of glue.

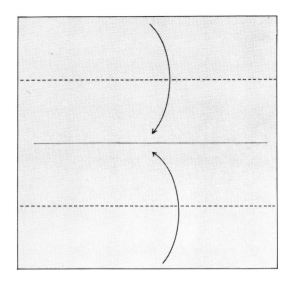

Figure 86. Dining table

Dining Table
Basic square.

1. Find the centre of the paper by lightly creasing it in half. Fold outer edges, top and bottom, forward to meet on this line.

2. Repeat the fold by bringing the top and bottom edges forward to the centre again.

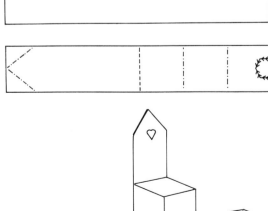

Figure 87. Chair and cushion

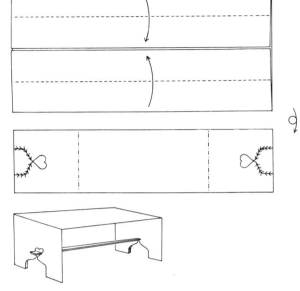

3. Turn the model over and make decorative cuts at each end. Crease and fold the ends to the back to form the legs of the table. Cut a small hole in the heart decoration large enough for a small bar made from a roll of paper to fit — this will keep the table rigid.

4. Finished model.

Paper $8\frac{1}{2} \times 8\frac{1}{2}$. Model $4\frac{1}{2} \times 2$.

Chair and Cushion
Basic square.

1. Cut a square of paper in half. Fold the resulting rectangle into three by folding the side panels over the centre one.

2. Crease and fold the strip into half and then one of the halves into thirds taking care to follow the direction indicated by the lines — taking the centre fold forward and the other two to the back. Fold the two end corners of the long section to the back and cut out a small section at the other end as a decoration.

3. Bring the chair into a standing position, and if necessary apply a small blob of glue to the back section.

4. Make a small cushion to fit the seat, as shown in diagram 49.

Paper $8\frac{1}{2} \times 4\frac{1}{2}$ for Chair. Model 4×1.
Paper 3×3 for Cushion. Model 1×1.

CHAPTER 9

Cards for Invitations and Announcements

The making of one's own invitation cards can give extra pleasure to both the party-giver and the guest. Suitable announcement cards are sometimes difficult to find to express individual messages. I have therefore made a collection of a few models which I considered suitable — you doubtless will be able to create and/or adapt others.

I suggest that you use heavy quality deckle edged paper for the announcement cards, and in most instances tissue paper for the models attached to them. For the invitation cards coloured paper is fun, and the plain side has been kept in our examples for the writing.

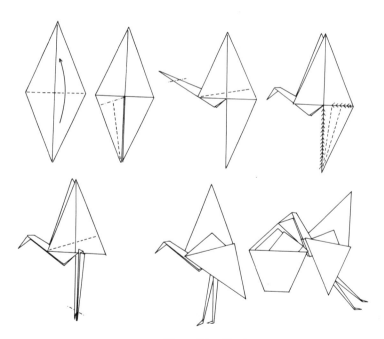

Figure 88. Stork

Stork
Basic fold seven.
1. Crease fold upper top flap down to meet lower points. Return to original position.
2. Crease fold for slender neck by bringing edge of lower left flap over to centre. Flatten

again and repeat crease on under flap. Crease fold for shoulder by taking the whole of the left-hand flap out and up to the left — flatten again.
3. Fold for neck by first taking left flap up to left in a pocket fold on crease line made and

then narrow the neck by folding the lower sides in to the centre on crease fold made in figure 2. Crease for head and make a pocket fold on line indicated. Make second crease fold on wing as shown, and flatten.

4. Separate the lower right-hand fold by cutting from the lower tip to the centre of the model on line indicated. Cut along three-quarters of the flaps on first crease line shown, and crease fold legs in half — top leg forward and lower leg to the back — and then in half again.

5. Pocket or hood fold feet and legs depending on whether you wish the stork to have arrived, or be on its way, and bring top wing down.

6. Drawing of standing model.

7. Drawing of flying model.

A small basket bearing an announcement card can be suspended from the beak of the stork.

Paper 4 × 4. Model 4 × 2½.

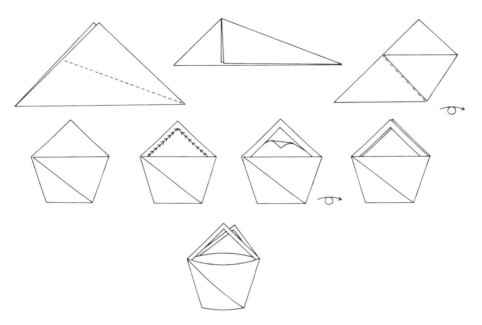

Figure 89. Basket

Basket (As carried by the stork on the announcement card)
Basic fold two.

1. Turn basic fold to position shown.

2. Take the top points forward and down to meet the lower edge — crease lightly because the sole purpose of this crease is to establish the point for the next fold. Open out to basic fold again.

3. Fold right-hand point over to meet earlier crease fold.

4. Turn model and repeat the movement.

5. Cut carefully along the lines indicated, through both layers of paper, to make the handles.

6. Fold flap forward and tuck between the outer layers.

7. Turn model and repeat the movement.

8. The finished model.

The model, if made in waxed paper with the handles not cut but the flaps tucked in, makes an excellent drinking cup.

Paper 8½ × 8½ makes cup 3½ in. high with a diameter of 3 in.

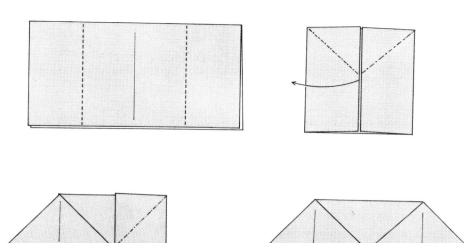

Figure 90. Simple house

Simple House

Basic fold one.

1. Bring basic fold to position shown. Fold left- and right-hand sides forward to meet in the centre.

2. Crease and fold inner points forward and down on lines shown. Open out the fold from the base and take the centre to the outside. This movement will cause the top fold to fall into a roof shape.

3. This diagram shows one end opened.

4. When house is fully opened, draw in windows and doors.

This is a flat house designed for pasting on to cards as part of the scenery, or for use on an invitation card.

Paper $8\frac{1}{2} \times 8\frac{1}{2}$. Model $8\frac{1}{2} \times 4\frac{1}{4}$.

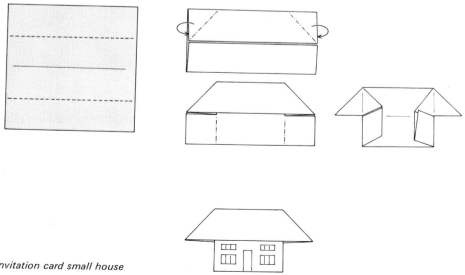

Figure 91. Invitation card small house

Invitation card — Small House

Basic square.

1. To find the centre, lightly fold the paper in half. Fold upper and lower edges in to meet this crease.
2. Crease and pocket fold the top left- and right-hand corners.
3. Fold the left- and right-hand sides to the back of the model.
4. Decorate the front of the house.
5. Turn the model over, open out the flaps and use the inside section to write on.
Paper $8\frac{1}{2} \times 8\frac{1}{2}$ makes model $8\frac{1}{2} \times 4\frac{1}{4}$.

Invitation card — Piglet

1. Pig as already made in Chapter Six.
2. Open for writing.

Open out model of pig along the backbone and use the open space for writing invitation on. When writing is completed, close model and refold tail.

Invitation card — Boat

Basic fold two, with wrong side of paper towards you.

1. Crease fold on line shown, taking the crease both ways.
2. Hood fold on crease line.
3. Crease fold bottom of hull. Cut along line indicated for sail and pennant.
4. To make the model stand cut along base line as indicated. This will also facilitate opening the model to enable it to be used as an invitation card.
5. Boat shown opened for use as a card or letterette.
Paper 6×6. Model $5 \times 5\frac{1}{2}$.

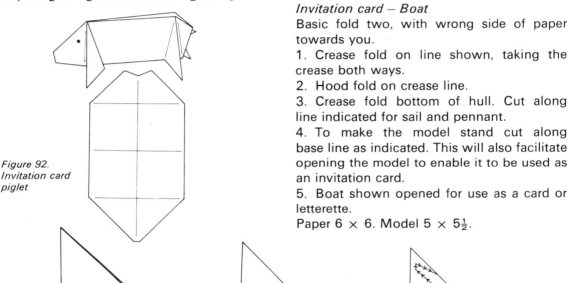

Figure 92. Invitation card piglet

Figure 93. Invitation card boat

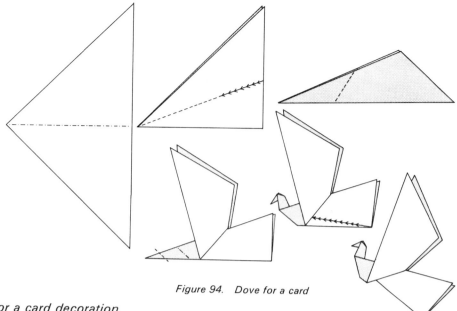

Figure 94. Dove for a card

Dove for a card decoration
Triangle of fine paper.
1. Cut a square of paper into four equal triangles. With the right side of the paper towards you, crease fold in half by taking the lower half back and up to meet the top half.
2. Fold the paper in half. Crease fold and cut on lines indicated.
3. Fold down the top points to the outside of the model, thus exposing the in or wrong side of the paper. Crease fold on line shown.
4. Fold back the wings on crease lines. Crease fold on lines shown.
5. Make a pocket fold for the neck and another for the head. Cut along line indicated and remove the paper.
6. Finished bird.
   Glue a flight of these birds, made in a pale paper, to a brightly-coloured card.
Paper 4 × 4 makes four birds, $1\frac{1}{2}$ × $2\frac{1}{2}$.

Variation of bird in flight — to be used on a card
Basic fold two.
1. With the right side of the paper on the outside, turn the basic fold to the position shown.
2. Crease fold and cut along lines indicated.
3. Make a pocket fold for the head. Fold the front wing down and the back wing up.
Fasten to a card.
Paper 2 × 2. Model $3\frac{1}{2}$ × $1\frac{1}{2}$.

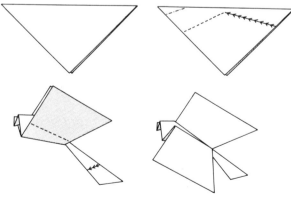

Figure 95.
Variation of bird in flight

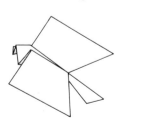

CHAPTER 10

Hallowe'en Decorations

The party decorations include:
Big-eared Bat
Blow-up Devil
Two-headed Cat (To be used as a mobile)
Jack-O-Lantern
Rattle

Dragon
Devil's Mask
Owl
Witch
    When made in dark or psychedelic colours these models are the greatest fun.

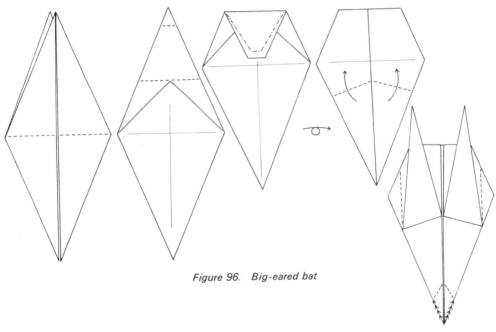

Figure 96. Big-eared bat

Big-eared Bat
Compound figure using two squares. Basic fold seven for body.
1. Fold upper top forward and down.
2. Make two crease folds on top points where indicated and fold forward and down.
3. Crease fold firmly and then fold sides of point under along lines shown. Turn point under again, thus making this section small but retaining its shape.

4. Turn model over and fold up the top two lower flaps. Press firmly.
5. Cut along outer edges of remaining lower flap as indicated and crease fold the pieces out. Crease and fold sides forward and in behind the ears.
6. This is the back of the first half-turn model over.
7. Front of bat.

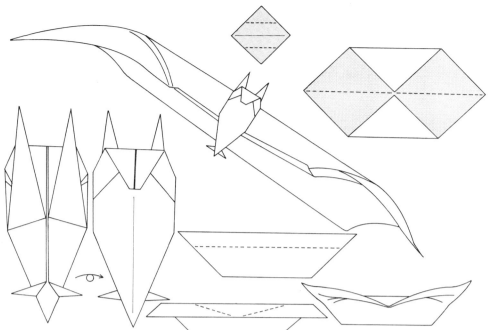

Wings:

Basic square four times size of square used for body of bat.

1. Turn to position shown. Crease fold as indicated.

2. Fold upper and lower points to centre.

3. Fold in half by bringing top section forward and down over lower. Crease partially but firmly on lines shown, bringing top edge of model forward and down.

4. Crease firmly and fold centre top section to the back.

5. Shape a little and glue wings to back of body.

6. Finished model.

Paper — body 8 × 8
Paper — wings 4 × 4 } Model 11 × 3½

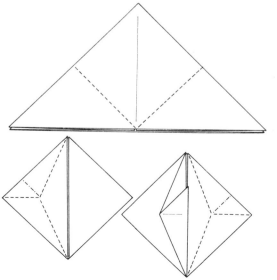

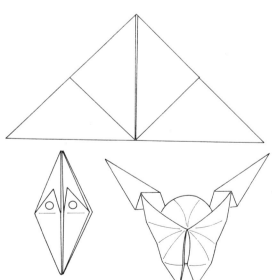

Figure 97. Blow-up devil

69

Blow-up Devil
Basic fold three.

1. Bring basic fold to position shown. Crease fold the top flaps of both left and right sides to the centre.

2. Make the folds. Turn the model and repeat on the other side.

3. Make careful crease folds by bringing both upper and lower sides forward to centre, and make short horizontal creases on the outer points. Take care with these creases.

4. Lift outer corners, and by gentle pressure push the folds into position shown. Turn the model over and repeat until both sides are the same.

5. Holding the model in the horizontal position — with small points above and below — hold the two lower points between your thumbs and the first fingers and blow up the devil. The inner points of the top foldings will open up. It is advisable to use a reasonably light-weight paper for the blow-up models — heavy tissue or light-weight copy paper.

6. Completed model.

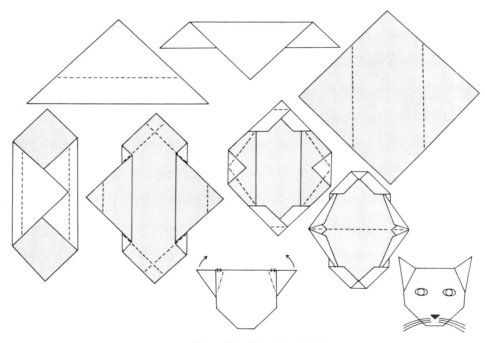

Figure 98. Two-headed cat

Two-headed Cat (to be used as a mobile)
Basic fold two.

1. Turn basic fold to position shown, keeping the right side of the paper towards you.

2. Fold down top tips of paper on line shown.

3. Open out paper.

4. Fold in sides of paper on previous crease folds. Crease fold on lines shown.

5. Fold inner points out on crease folds. Crease fold on lines shown.

6. Make folds on crease folds. Crease fold on lines shown.

7. Crease fold model in half by taking the top section forward and down over the lower one.

8. Fold the model in half. Crease fold and cut on lines indicated.

9. Make pocket folds with ears — you will find that the small cut allows the ears to be lifted slightly.

Add whiskers, draw in nose and eyes. The cat should be reinforced at stage 7 if it is to be suspended.

Paper $4\frac{1}{2} \times 4\frac{1}{2}$. Model 3×2.

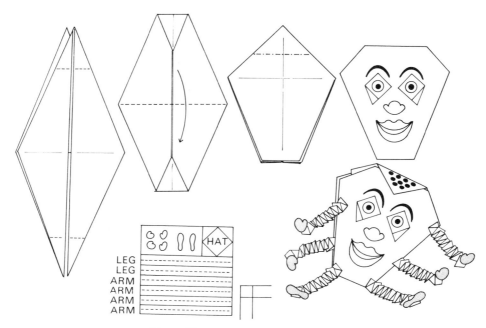

Figure 99. Jack-O-Lantern/Clown

Jack-O-Lantern/Clown

Basic fold seven, and square for limbs and hat.

1. Turn basic fold to position indicated. Crease fold on lines shown.
2. Fold top points, one to the back and one to the front. Hood fold lower points on crease lines. Crease fold on lines shown.
3. Bring top flaps down — one to the front and one to the back.
4. For firmness, put small cocktail sticks, lightly smeared with glue, in the corners and then glue the chin ends of the lantern together. Decorate to taste.
5. From a square of paper cut strips for arms and legs, shapes for feet, hands and hat.
6. Make legs by joining the ends of two strips as shown and folding them alternately one over the other.
7. Open out model. Glue hat with hanging thread affixed and limbs in position.

Paper 8 × 8. Model 4 × 3.

Square for limbs $8\frac{1}{2} \times 8\frac{1}{2}$.

Rattle

Basic fold three.

1. Crease fold right- and left-hand corners of top layers only forward on lines shown.
2. Fold firmly on crease lines. Turn the model over and repeat on the other side.
3. Crease firmly left- and right-hand corners bringing them forward to meet in the centre.
4. Crease fold very firmly all the layers of the top point — both to the back and to the front.
5. Turn the model over and repeat the movements. Fold on crease lines.
6. Fold the split points down on the crease folds already made — crease again on the diagonal line indicated and secure them by tucking them in between the layers of the centre point. Turn model and repeat the movements.
7. The model is now ready for inflating — blow lightly and dryly into the bottom — the firm crease folds made in fold 4 will cause the

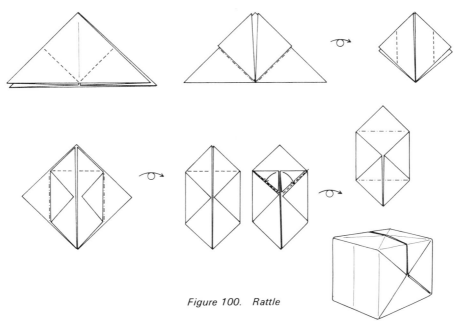

Figure 100.   Rattle

model to open into a square box-like shape, (8).

Amusing Caracas-type rattles can be made with this folding. Use papers of different textures and insert a few grains of rice, split or whole dried peas or other similar dried seeds. To avoid damaging and enlarging the opening it is better to insert these at stage three of the folding. The rattle can be used as a ball; in this case seal the folded ends with a small shape of gummed paper. Coloured spots can be added to the sides to turn it into a die.

Paper 6×6. Model $1\frac{1}{2} \times 1\frac{1}{2}$.

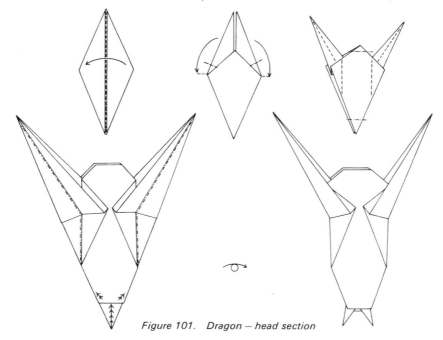

Figure 101.   Dragon — head section

Dragon
Head Section:
Basic fold seven.
1. Crease and fold top right flap over to the left, and bottom left under to the right.
2. Crease fold firmly on lines shown.
3. Lift the lower flaps out to their respective sides using previous crease folds. Crease fold on lines shown.

4. Fold top flap of nose section under and cut remaining layer on line indicated. Fold sides forward and continue the fold to the tips of the ears. Fold top of head section in.
5. Turn model over and repeat folds, making a slight adjustment to the nose fold by folding up the cut ends and bringing them down again at an angle.
Paper 8 × 8. Head size 7 × 5.

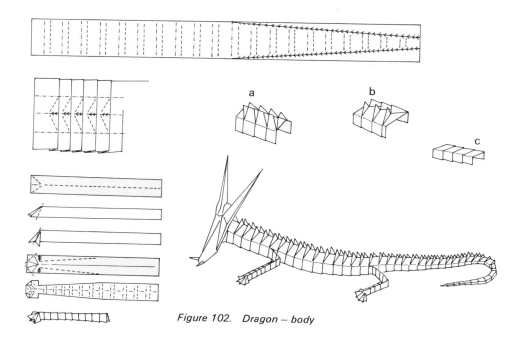

Figure 102. Dragon – body

Body:
1. Cut a rectangle of paper to the desired length. Taper for the tail. Concertina pleat at the distances indicated.
2. When pleating has been completed crease and fold the body on lines shown. Cut small sections along spine as indicated.
3. a and b show the way to achieve shape in the body: the section near the head (a) is arched. The section in the middle of the body (b) is fatter and flatter, and the tail section (c) is not cut but is folded in a squarer

fashion.
4. You will need four strips for the legs — one for each. Crease fold on lines shown, and fold legs in half and pocket fold the ends.
5. Crease fold the foot end again.
6. Fold on crease lines.
7. Cut and then crease on lines indicated.
8. Concertina fold at distances indicated.
9. Finished leg. Make three others, and glue into place.
10. Add the head to the body and your dragon is ready.

Devil's Mask

Basic fold two.

1. Turn basic fold to position shown. Crease fold left- and right-hand corners forward to meet at lower centre point.

2. Make the fold and crease fold on lines indicated back and up to form ears, being careful to crease from outer corners and to make folds equal.

3. Make crease fold to bring left and right outer points to centre, halving the ears as shown.

4. Complete the fold and round off the face by folding in head point, folding up chin point and then folding in for jaw line.

5. Make the folds firmly and then turn model over.

6. Draw a face on your devil and if you wish to hang him, thread a length of thread from the base of one ear to the other.

Paper 4 × 4. Model 1½ × 3.

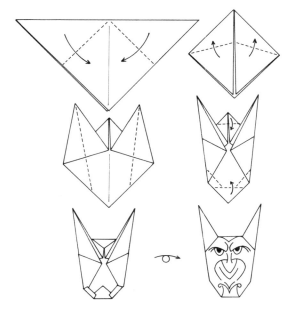

Figure 103. Devil's mask

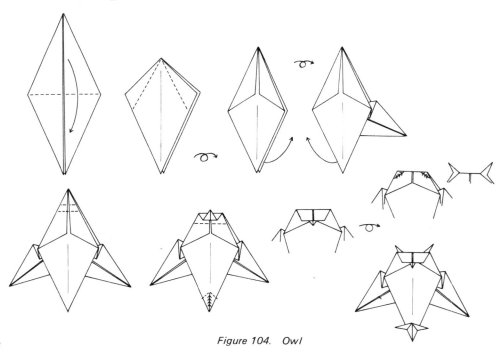

Figure 104. Owl

Owl

Basic fold seven.

1. Crease fold in centre.

2. Fold top flaps down, one to the front and the other to the rear.

3. Fold in sides on crease lines shown, first on the front side. Turn model over and repeat.

4. Lift the right centre section up and out to form a wing. Take careful note of the angle shown.

5. Repeat on other side. Two wings have now been formed. Crease fold for head.
6. Begin to shape the head by making two folds on lines shown. Cut lower top layer of lower central section and fold out to form feet.

Crease fold again for head (6a).
7. Turn model over and make cuts on lines indicated. Lift to form ears, (7a).
8. Finished model.
Paper $4\frac{1}{2} \times 4\frac{1}{2}$. Model 4×3.

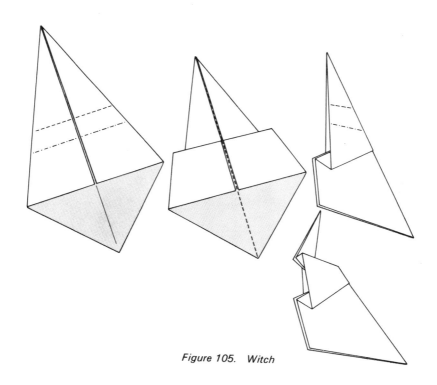

Figure 105. Witch

Witch

Basic fold four.

1. Turn basic fold to position shown. Make crease folds, the upper crease forward and the lower crease back.
2. Make folds as shown. Crease fold on line shown.
3. Fold in half by bringing right side over to the left. Make crease folds as shown.
4. Make two pocket folds on lines indicated. The witch is now ready to mount her broomstick. Paper 6×6. Model 6×3.

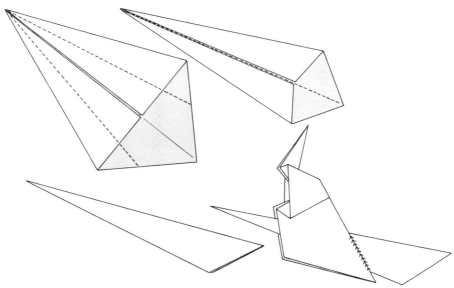

Figure 106. Broomstick

Broomstick
Basic fold four.
1. Place basic form in position shown. Make crease folds on lines shown.
2. Fold long sides to centre.
3. Fold in half, keeping closed edge of model to the top.

4. Make an appropriately sized slit in the cape of the witch and mount her on her broomstick. If the model is to be used hanging a small blob of glue is used to keep the broomstick in position. Finished model is about one third of original paper size.
Paper 6 × 6. Model 8 × 1.

CHAPTER 11

Nativity Scene

For this chapter I have used both simple and compound models, so that the making of the scene of the Nativity can be a group activity as befits the occasion. The models, if you use paper of the recommended size, are in proportion.

To make a complete scene you will need:

Screen: four pieces of heavy quality paper 20 × 20, and four pieces 8 × 8.*

Palm tree: the trunk paper 2 × 8; the tree-top paper 15 × 10.

Joseph: one piece 7 × 7.

Virgin Mary: for the body one piece 7 × 7; for the head 2 × 2; for the head shawl 3½ × 2 or for simpler version 2½ × 2½.

Baby: 3½ × 3½.

Crib: 3½ × 4½.

Shepherds: 7 × 7.†

Ox (compound): two pieces 7 × 7.

Ass (compound): two pieces 7 × 7.

Lamb: Head section 3½ × 3½. Rear section 4½ × 4½.

Arrange all on a base of convenient shape for the grouping of your choice.

Figure 107.   Nativity Scene

* Prepare Screen as for Base of Easter Scene (Page 34).
† The folding pattern for the shepherds is exactly the same as for Joseph. The shepherds are arranged within the group in a kneeling position while Joseph remains standing. A more colourful scene can be made if different coloured papers are used for each of the shepherds.

Palm tree

1. Fold the 2 × 8 paper for the trunk in half. Cut away the sides in the manner shown.
2. Fold the 15 × 10 paper for the top of the tree in half and cut this out also in the manner shown. Curl the 'branches' by pulling them gently over a knife. Glue them to the top of the trunk.

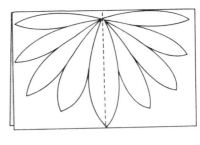

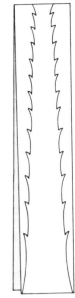

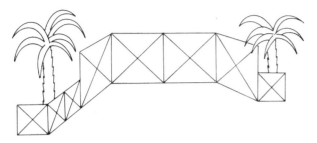

Figure 108. Background

Figure 109. Palm tree

Joseph

Square of paper with plain side to the front.
1. Fold the square into four lengthwise and cut off one section. Crease fold into three. Crease fold in band on right-hand edge.
2. Wrap sides to centre bringing coloured side to the outside and contrasting band to the front. Crease fold on lines shown.
3. Open model out and pleat fold lower crease, taking the lowest forward and up. Fold top forward and in on crease line.
4. Make crease fold on lines shown.
5. Put main model aside and make the head section from strip cut off from original square. With coloured side of paper uppermost — for you will want the head to be on the plain side to contrast with the body and head shawl sections — cut along lines shown. Crease fold where indicated.
6. Fold the head section in a rolling fashion — starting with small fold indicated in diagram 5, from right to left.
7. Use this strip for an inner scarf.
8. Wrap the strip around the head in manner indicated and glue in position.
9. Place head section in neck opening and wrap body around it.

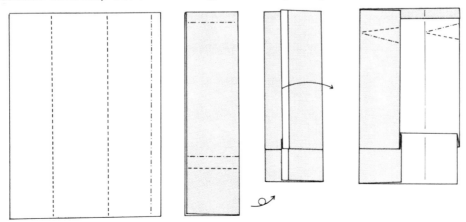

Figure 110. Joseph

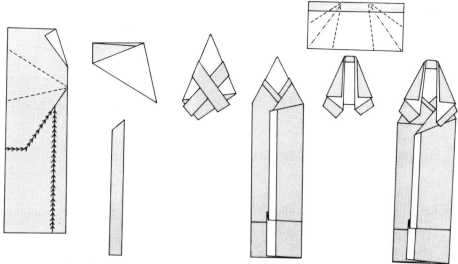

10. From a rectangle of paper the same width and half as long as the strip used for the head section, fold in the top edge and crease fold as shown.

11. Fold head shawl as shown.

12. Model completed.
This is the basic form used for the shepherds and with a slight variation for the nurse in Chapter Eight.
Paper 7 × 7. Model 6½ × 2.

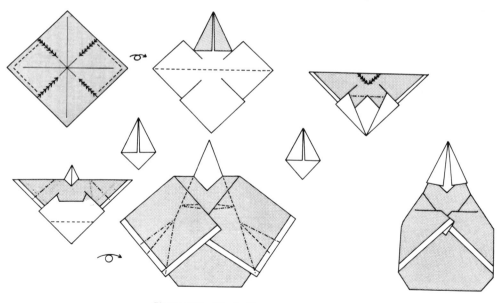

Figure 111. Virgin Mary

Virgin Mary
Basic square 7 × 7 for body.
Basic square 2 × 2 for head.
Rectangle for head 3½ × 2, or
Square for head shawl 2½ × 2½.
1. With the coloured side of the paper to the front, crease fold the paper into quarters and eighths — making all creases to the back. Cut along four of the crease lines for distance shown (two thirds). Fold forward

a narrow band along the outer edges of the right- and left-hand sections.

2. Turn paper over and fold in the sides of the top point. Make head of pale coloured paper (2a) and slip it over the folded point shown in diagram 2 – the broad point being on the coloured side of the paper. Crease and fold the model in half by bringing the top forward and down to meet the bottom.

3. This diagram shows the head section in position. Crease fold under on line indicated. Cut out small triangle on lines shown.

4. Thread the head section under and through the opening made previously. Crease fold the right- and left-hand points both to the back and to the front. Crease fold the lower tip up and forward. Turn model over.

5. Lift the side corners up and flatten into squares using the crease folds made previously. Crease and fold along lines indicated to shape the figure taking the sides to the back. Lift the front by taking two small pleat folds on front edges.

6. Complete the figure by adding a head shawl (7) – this can be made in the style designed for Joseph or can be a simple white one similar in shape to the section used for the head.

Paper 7 × 7. Model $3\frac{1}{2}$ × $4\frac{1}{2}$.

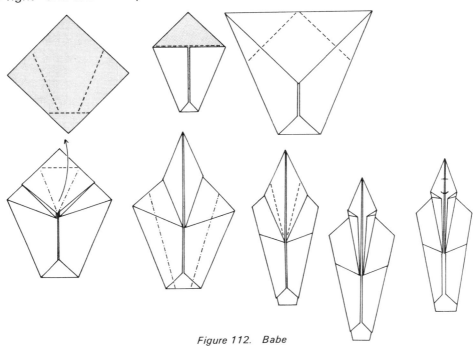

Figure 112. Babe

Babe

Basic square.

1. Crease fold on lines shown – all forward.
2. Complete folds. Crease fold on line shown.
3. Fold top point down. Crease fold top on lines shown.
4. Pocket fold top points forward and in. Crease fold on lines shown.
5. Fold in sides of the outer points of the head section. Lift centre point out and up as though making Basic Fold Seven.

Crease fold to the back on lines shown.

6. Fold sides to the back on crease lines. Crease fold sides of head section forward to the front.
7. Fold sides of head section to the front.
8. Lift centre opening of head section and slip in small circle for face. Shape the model a little by opening up the folds slightly.

Paper $3\frac{1}{2}$ × $3\frac{1}{2}$. Model $2\frac{1}{2}$ × 1.

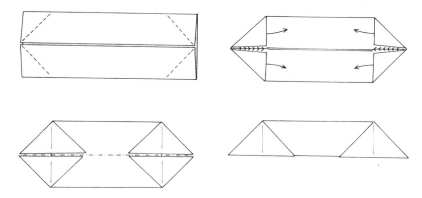

Figure 113. Crib

Crib

Basic square.

1. Fold square into four, lengthwise, and cut off one piece to form a rectangle. Crease fold the rectangle into half and open out again. Fold the top and bottom edges to the centre line. Crease fold all four corners both to the back and to the front.
2. Fold the corners forward. Cut along lines indicated.
3. Lift corners and flatten so that they form triangles, as shown. Fold the model in half by taking the lower part under and up to meet the top.
4. Tuck the front flaps, both left and right, into the back ones to form the end of the crib. This will bring the legs down into position.

Paper $3\frac{1}{2} \times 4\frac{1}{2}$. Model $3 \times 1\frac{1}{2}$.

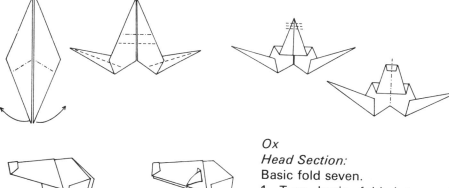

Figure 114. Ox – head section

Ox

Head Section:

Basic fold seven.

1. Turn basic fold into position shown. Pocket fold lower points — one out to the right and the other to the left. Bring the top of the folds above the horizontal.
2. Crease and fold these flaps on lines shown, taking the front ones forward and the others to the back. Pleat fold the top point on lines indicated.
3. Crease and fold the top tip forward and down to form the nose.
4. Fold the model in half by taking the right-

hand point back and behind to meet the left.

5. Crease fold for legs in positions shown. From the top layer of paper forming the head, cut horns and a little 'hair'.

6. Make double pocket folds on the legs and hood folds for the feet.
Paper 7 × 7. Head of model $5\frac{1}{2}$ × $3\frac{1}{2}$.

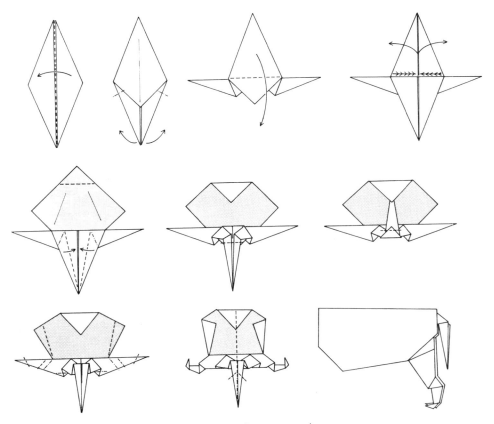

Figure 115. Ox — rear section

Rear Section:
Basic fold seven.

1. Turn the basic fold to position shown.

2. Fold top right-hand flap across to the left and rear left-hand section to the right.

3. Pocket fold the lower points to the side, one to the left and one to the right. Keep the top of the folds horizontal. Bring the top fold down on the line indicated.

4. Cut from open centre to outside edges of the top point and open out to form a diamond shape.

5. Crease fold on lines shown, folding the top point forward and down and the sides of the lower point to the centre, being careful to flatten out the top section of it.

6. Fold both of the lower points forward and in on line shown, and top point down.

7. Fold both of these points down again for the tail.

8. Crease and fold on lines shown, folding sides forward and across. Hood and pocket fold for legs and hood fold for feet.

9. Make a pocket fold on tail section on line shown.

10. Fold model in half by bringing the right side over to the left.

When both sections have been completed insert the rear section into the front and glue them together.
Paper 7 × 7. Rear portion of model 4 × 3.

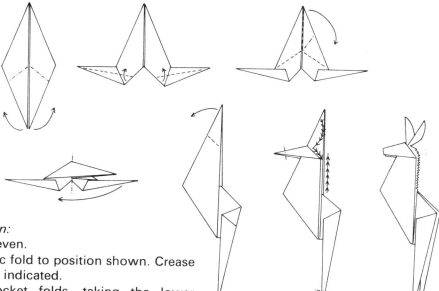

Ass

Head Section:
Basic fold seven.

1. Turn basic fold to position shown. Crease fold on lines indicated.

2. Make pocket folds, taking the lower points to their respective sides. Crease fold on lines shown, taking the front sections forward and up and the back section to the back and up.

3. Fold outer sections on crease lines made previously. Crease fold the top point on lines indicated, taking the point forward and down along the edge of the hidden triangle. Careful creasing in this way will keep the back of the Ass free from other, unwanted creases.

4. Bring the top tip forward and down using the crease lines already made. Fold the

Figure 116. Ass — head section

model in half by bringing the right-hand point behind and across to meet that on the left. A hood fold will in fact have been made.

5. Half turn the model and crease and hood fold the outer layer of the upper point out to the left.

6. Crease and fold in the point for nose and mark the cutting line for the ears.

7. Complete the head section by cutting out the shape for the ears and making a fringe for the mane.

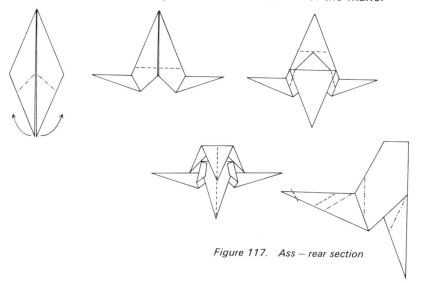

Figure 117. Ass — rear section

83

Rear Section:

Basic fold seven.

1. Turn basic fold to position shown. Crease fold on lines indicated.

2. Pocket fold bottom points out to sides on crease fold already made. Crease and fold top point forward and down on line shown.

3. Crease and fold the top layer of inner points forward and in on lines indicated. Crease and fold top point forward and down on line indicated.

4. Fold the model in half by folding the right-hand side forward and over to meet the left.

5. Crease fold on lines shown, making the leg and tail crease both forwards and to the back.

6. Half turn the model and make a double pocket fold for the leg and a hood fold for the foot. Pocket fold the tail. Turn the crease on the body section under. Turn model and repeat leg and body folds.

To complete the model insert the rear section into the front and glue together.

Head paper 7 × 7 } Finished model 4½ × 4.
Rear paper 7 × 7 }

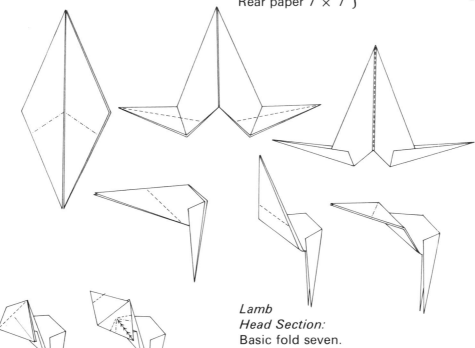

Lamb

Head Section:

Basic fold seven.

1. Turn basic fold to position indicated. Crease fold on lines shown.

2. Pocket fold lower points out to their respective sides. Crease fold on lines shown.

3. Fold to front and back on crease lines. Crease fold model in centre.

4. Fold model in half by bringing right side over to the left. Crease fold on line shown.

5. Fold the left point up on crease line and crease on line shown.

6. Fold the head down on crease fold. Crease on line shown.

7. Form the head by opening the fold and bringing it forward and down. Crease fold,

Figure 118. Lamb — head section

84

to the back, on the line shown.

8. Fold top layer of head paper up on crease line and crease fold the tip. Cut along line indicated and crease fold on lines shown.

9. Fold out the ears. Fold down the top tip. Make crease folds on front legs.

10. Fold down the head section as indicated. Make double pocket folds on each leg.

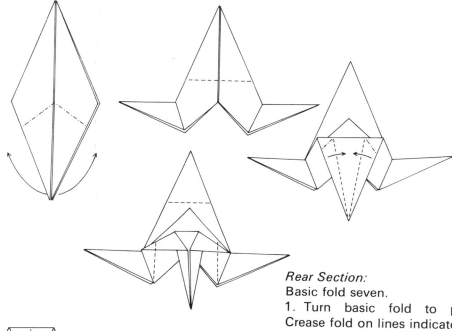

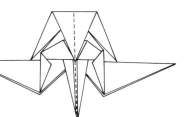

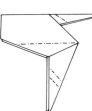

Rear Section:
Basic fold seven.

1. Turn basic fold to position shown. Crease fold on lines indicated.

2. Pocket fold lower points out to their respective sides. Crease fold on lines shown.

3. Fold top flap forward and down. Crease fold on lines shown.

4. Fold the sides of the lower point forward to the centre, carefully flattening the tops into the triangles shown.

5. Fold inner sides to centre along crease folds. Fold top tip forward and down. Crease fold model in half.

6. Fold model in half by taking the right side point across to meet that on the left. Crease fold on lines shown – on tail and legs forward and on the body to the back. Repeat on the other side.

7. Pocket fold for the tail. Double pocket fold the legs. Fold body section under on lines shown.

8. Model completed.

Insert rear section into the front and glue together.

Head paper $3\frac{1}{2} \times 3\frac{1}{2}$. } Completed model
Rear paper $4\frac{1}{2} \times 4\frac{1}{2}$. } 3 × 2.

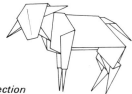

Figure 119. Lamb – rear section

CHAPTER 12

Ideas for Christmas Decorations

For this festive season I have included table decorations, fans, party hats, gift wrappings, candle holders and napkin folds.

REINDEER AND SLEIGH.

A good scene for the table centre is one of reindeer pulling a sleigh. To make these models you will need:

Base: a rectangle of card $22\frac{1}{2} \times 6\frac{1}{4}$.
Base Cover: four squares of stiff paper 16×16.
Sleigh: brown paper 10×10.
Harness: a strip of red paper $\frac{1}{4} \times 2$ for the noseband. $4\frac{3}{4} \times \frac{1}{2}$ for the bellyband. Two lengths of red ribbon 30 inches long for the reins.
Reindeer (two): you will need for each two squares of tough gold paper 10×10.
Small Parcels: made from paper approximately $2\frac{1}{2} \times 2\frac{1}{2}$.

Base:
1. Choose heavy card for under base

$22\frac{1}{2} \times 6\frac{1}{4}$.
2. From four squares of heavy paper, each square being 16×16, make four bases as for the Easter scene, Chapter Five. Interlock them as shown.
3. Cut paper for harness and ribbon for reins.

Sleigh:
1. Bed as in Chapter Eight.
2. Open out and curl under the headboard. Turn the legs into runners, by cutting where indicated. Fold the runners flat.

Reindeer:
Head Section:
Basic fold seven.
1. Turn basic fold to position shown. Crease fold on lines indicated.
2. Pocket fold lower points out to their respective sides on lines indicated. Crease fold to narrow these sections for legs by halving. Take the front sections of the point forward, and the back sections to the

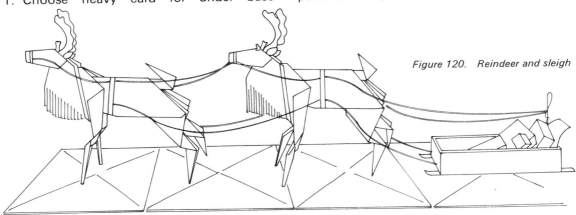

Figure 120. Reindeer and sleigh

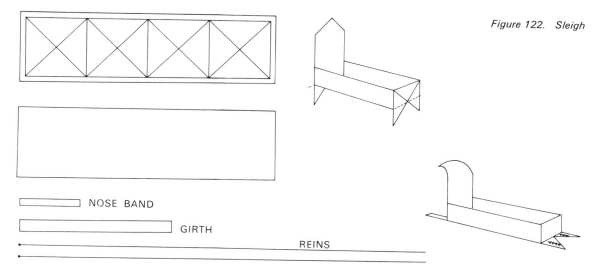

Figure 122. Sleigh

NOSE BAND

GIRTH

REINS

Figure 121. Base

back.

3. Crease fold carefully along the line shown.
4. Fold the two top points forward, down and across on the crease line already made.
5. Turn model over. Cut top layer, single sheet of paper along lines indicated. Crease fold left side of triangle. Fold model in half by bringing the right-hand point forward and across to meet the left. This will in fact bring about a hood fold.
6. Crease fold on lines indicated, twice on the legs and twice on the head section.
7. Hood fold the outer point down to form the head. Fold in nose section. Draw in shape for the antlers. Cut off section to round off neck. Make two hood folds on the legs.
8. Complete the head of the animal by cutting out the antlers and fringing the neck hair.

Paper for rear 10 × 10 } Finished model
Paper for head 10 × 10 ∫ $5\frac{1}{2} \times 6\frac{3}{4}$.

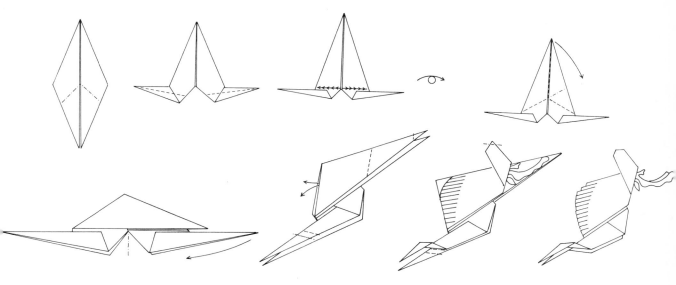

Figure 123. Reindeer — head section

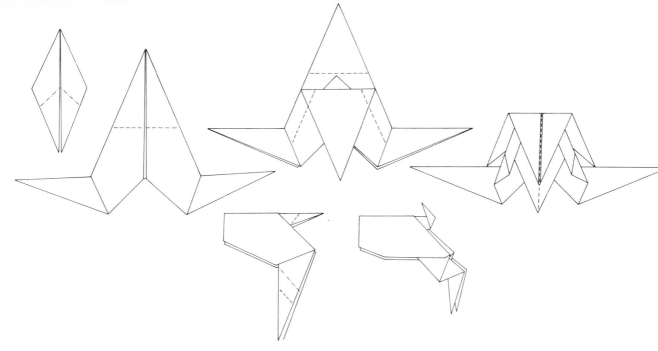

Figure 124. Reindeer – rear section

Rear Section:

Basic fold seven.

1. Turn basic fold to position shown. Crease fold on lines indicated.

2. Pocket fold lower points out to their respective sides. Crease fold front layer of top point forward and down.

3. Fold legs carefully along the lines shown. Cut top layer, single sheet of paper, as indicated. Turn model over.

4. Crease fold on lines shown.

5. Folding in from right, bring top points forward and across. Fold model in half by bringing right point under to meet left. This forms hood fold and releases cut edges for shaping of chest.

6. Hood fold tail up. Double pocket fold legs on crease folds.

7. Glue head and rear sections together.

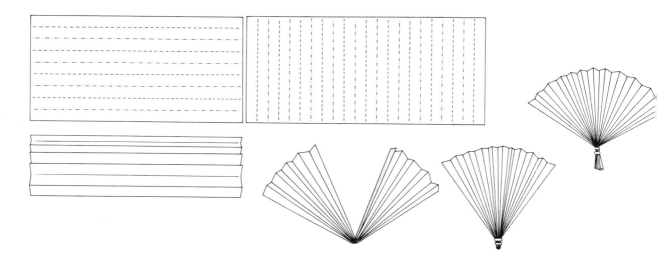

Figure 125. Simple fans

Simple Fans

Simple fans are made from successive foldings and the making of them is very useful practice for accuracy of creasing.

These fans can also be used as skirts for dolls, wings for angels, mobiles and a myriad of other things — but only when the folding is immaculate.

I find it easier to make the first crease in the centre and then come forward. Return to the centre and then fold to back.

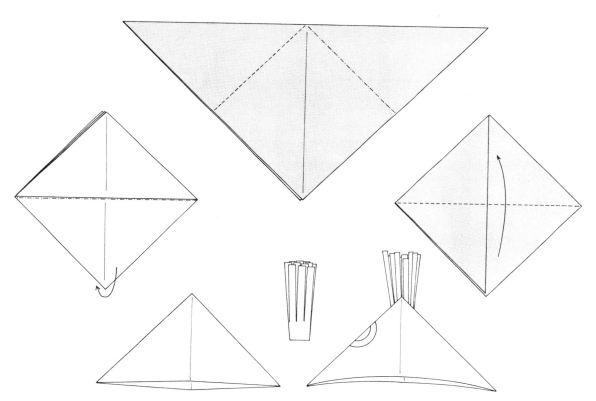

Figure 126. Hat — Napoleon

Hat — in the style of Napoleon

Basic fold two.

1. Turn the basic fold to the position shown. Crease and fold the left- and right-hand corners, one to the front and one to the back down to meet the lower point.
2. Crease and fold half of the lower points forward and up along the line shown.
3. Crease and fold remaining points back and up.
4. This diagram shows folds completed and hat ready for trimming.
5. Cut a short cockade from a rectangle of paper.
6. Glue the cockade into position and decorate the hat with medallions.

Paper $8\frac{1}{2} \times 8\frac{1}{2}$ allows a headband of approximately 10 in.

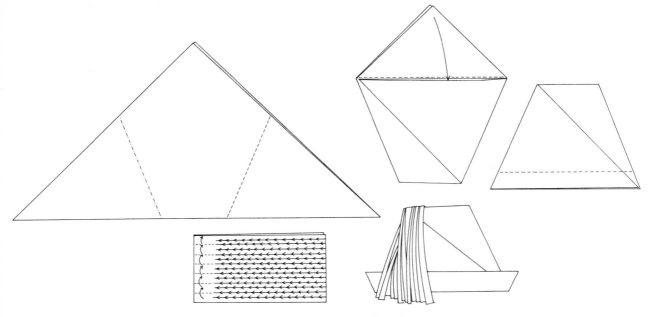

Figure 127. Hat — Bavarian

Hat — a Bavarian style

Basic fold two.

1. Bring the basic fold into the position shown, with the open points at the top. On the lines indicated, fold the sides across. The right-hand point is taken forward and across the front and the left-hand one to the back and across.

2. Fold in the top points by tucking them into the folds, one to the back and one to the front.

3. Fold down the edges to form a brim. The hat is now ready for trimming.

4. Make a tassel which will fall to the edge of the hat. Tuck the uncut end into the fold and secure it with a little blob of glue.

5. The finished hat.

Paper $8\frac{1}{2} \times 8\frac{1}{2}$ will make a headband of about 10 in.

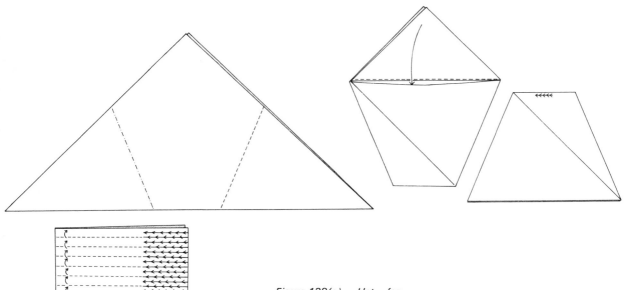

Figure 128(a). Hat — fez

Hat – in the style of a Fez
Basic fold two.
1. Turn the basic fold to the position shown, with the open ends at the top. Fold in the left- and right-hand sides, one to the back and one to the front, on lines indicated.
2. Fold down the two top points, one to the front and one to the back. Tuck these into the double folds.
3. Cut a small hole in the centre of the top for the tassel.
4. From a rectangle of paper, make a tassel as shown by cutting and then rolling it.
5. Insert the tassel into the hole made for it and glue into position.
6. Bring the tassel over and fix to the side of the hat.
Paper 8½ × 8½. Headband 10 in.

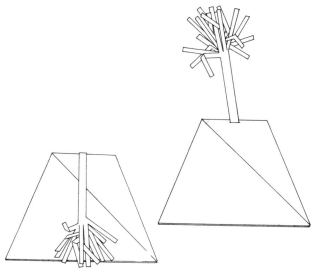

Figure 128(b).

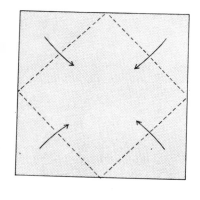

Figure 129. Gift wrapping

Simple ideas for gift wrapping
1. Make square for the top of the parcel. Crease and fold the corners to the centre.
2. Concertina crease the corners from the centre to the outside.

3. Creasing completed, turn the model over.
4. Fold the corners to the centre. The decoration is complete.
5. Shows finished model.
Paper 5 × 5. Finished model 2½ × 2½.

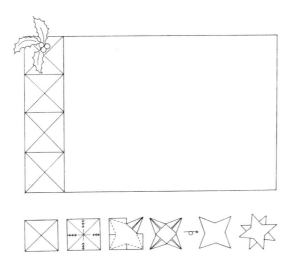

Figure 130. Table setting

Table Setting

Rectangle of paper the size of a table mat.

1. Place line of small 'bases' along one end. When calculating the size of these remember that they are reduced to one third of the size of paper used.
2. Make other bases for glasses and centre pieces.
3. Alternative decorations for mats are stars used singly or grouped. Fold a square in half diagonally, horizontally and vertically.
4. Cut along lines as indicated.
5. Fold in along cut lines to form a star.
6. Turn model over.
7. Make a second star in the same way but in a different colour and fix above the first one. The star is the size of the diagonal measurement of the original square.

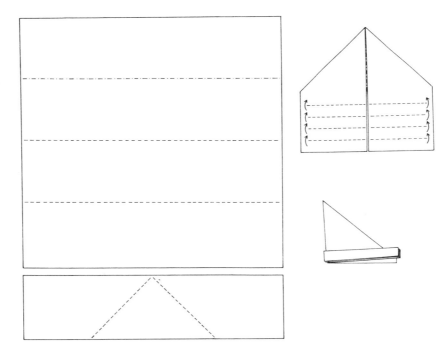

Figure 131. Napkin in boat form

Napkin in boat form for holding a roll

1. Fold napkin in half and in half again.
2. Fold forward diagonally on lines indicated.
3. Roll each side up separately as far as the corners.

4. Fold model in half with the rolled ends on outside and clip together. Models can be placed separately on plates or massed as a mini fleet in the centre of the table.

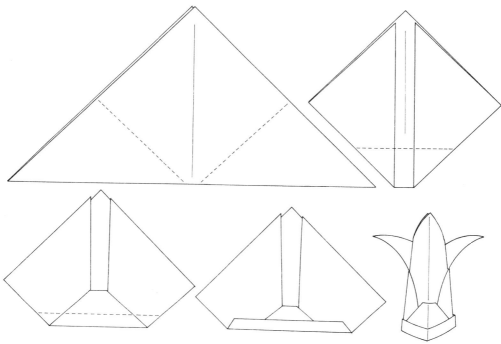

Figure 132. Napkin folded as a lily

Napkin folded as a lily

1. Fold the napkin in half diagonally keeping the folded edge at the bottom. Fold the side points in to meet a little short of the top.
2. Fold up the lower edge on line shown.
3. Fold up the lower edge again as indicated.
4. Crease fold the model by taking the sides round and overlapping them at the back.
5. Pull out the petals.

Napkin folded as a flower holder

1. Fold the napkin into half diagonally, keeping the folded edge at the top. Fold left- and right-hand corners to the centre.
2. Fold the two lower points partially up as indicated. Fold up the remaining point on line shown.

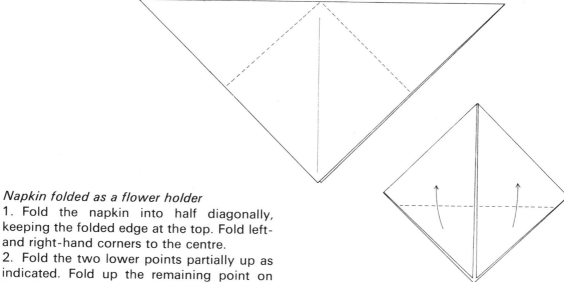

Figure 133(a). Napkin folded as a flower holder

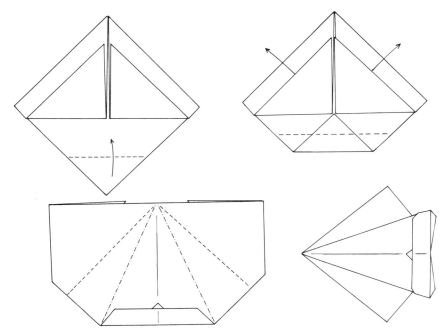

Figure 133(b).

3. Fold bottom edge up again leaving the point of the other tip showing. Lift out to their respective sides the two upper flaps, so that you have the outline as shown in diagram 4.

4. Fold sides to the back on lines shown, utilising the earlier folds as a base.

5. Lift the centre of the holder slightly to make space for the flower or small gift which it is to contain.

Decorative Ball

A decorative ball made from the interlocked bases described in Chapter Five. Small groups of flowers are tucked into the centre of some of the sections. The top section has been reinforced for hanging — it has a small circle of linen glued to the inside. The bottom has also been reinforced to take the weight of the tassel. Made with foil these balls are very decorative on the Christmas tree — in pastel colours they are very pretty when suspended in a nursery or on a crib.

Ballet Scene

An alternative table decoration, for which you will need a lakelike base, a selection of dancers in various poses, swans, cygnets and perhaps water lilies.

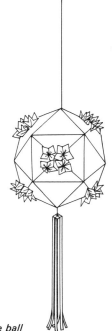

Figure 134. Decorative ball

Figure 135.   Ballet Scene

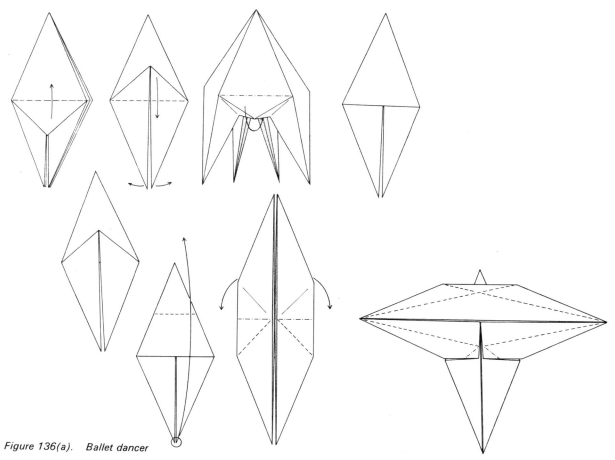

Figure 136(a).   Ballet dancer

95

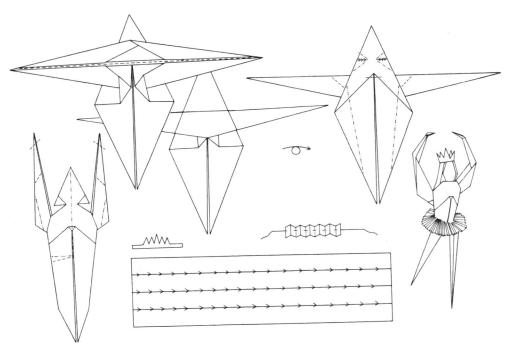

Figure 136(b).

Ballet dancer

Basic fold eight.

1 & 2. Crease fold small centre flap both up and down on line indicated.

3. Lift the two lower flaps out to their respective sides until it is possible to slip the small central flap under to the inside.

4. Close model again.

5. Turn model over and fold up small flap — this will be used for the bodice of the tutu.

6. Turn model over again and crease fold the top point forward and down on line indicated. This crease will facilitate the next fold.

7. Lift the upper pair of the lower flaps up and to the side until the centre sections are flat, being careful to flatten the triangle made by the lower flaps. Check the lines on the diagram carefully.

Crease and fold along lines shown, being careful to flatten the centre triangles which will appear.

8. Crease and fold the cross flaps in half by bringing top section forward and down over the bottom.

9. This diagram shows the folds completed.

10. Turn the model over. Crease and fold sides in, front inside to the back and back forward and inside — this is to make the slender legs. Hood fold arms on lines shown. Cut along lines indicated to shape for neck and head. Fold front section under and back to form the face. Pocket fold lower sections in to form the shoulders.

11. Crease and fold arms on lines indicated. First fold in section closest to the body to make the arm slender. Next pocket and hood fold arms.

12. Make and add crown. From a rectangle of paper cut narrow strips, pleat fold these and thread through with cotton to form a tutu. Different stances can be modelled by adjusting the angle of arms and legs.

13. Shape model by creasing slightly in the centre.

Paper $7\frac{1}{2} \times 7\frac{1}{2}$ makes Dancer $2\frac{1}{2} \times 6$ in.